LOVE, LIFE & MOVING PICTURES

Terence Sharkey

ಜಲ

Copyright © MMXVII Terence Sharkey. All rights reserved.
The right of Terence Sharkey to be identified as the author of this work has been asserted in accordance with the Copyright, Designs and Patents Act 1988.

Events, places and people have been transposed for literary purposes. It should not be supposed that the representation of any person living or dead has been sanctioned.

Every effort has been made to ensure the correct acknowledgement of courtesy and copyright material. Please contact the author if material has not been properly attributed.
sharkbytes@topmail.ie
http://www.lovelifeandmovingpictures.com

ISBN: 978-1508578321
ASIN: BoolJYEl6H2
Vers. 1/17

British Library Cataloguing in Publication Data.
A catalogue record for this book is available from the British Library.

First published in Kindle 2014

CreateSpace, An Amazon.com Company.

By the same author and soon to be republished in Kindle:
Jack the Ripper, 100 Years of Investigation.
Ward Lock, London.
Dorset Press, New York.

Contents

Foreword		v
Author		vii
Epigraph		ix
Chapter one	Audition	1
Chapter two	Location	11
Chapter three	Grand Hotel	25
Chapter four	Having a ball	39
Chapter five	Sincerity	49
Chapter six	Wheelus Field USAAF	55
Chapter seven	London pride	67
Chapter eight	The girl next door	89
Chapter nine	Ghosts without greasepaint	107
Chapter ten	And all that jazz	113
Chapter eleven	Margaret	129
Chapter twelve	Fallen idol	137
Chapter thirteen	Dream factory	143
Chapter fourteen	Picardie	151
Chapter fifteen	Adieu	163
Chapter sixteen	Epilogue	171
End note	Capt D.R. Griffiths	176
Bibliography		177
Index		178

Foreword

So. What have we here?

A romance? A technical film commentary? An historical look at mid-20th century London, its jazz clubs, its cruel Soho underworld? The backstage world behind London's West-End theatre curtain? How 19th century child-labour laws affected child-actors in the 20th? Snatches of biography of some 1950s film actors - ghosts, long-dead yet still familiar faces on today's television screens? Tales of theatre ghosts?

> **It is all these things but above all it is the story of a young actor who found unexpected romance on a foreign film location, where off-camera events were to be more dramatic than any taking place before the Technicolor camera on the sands of the Sahara.**

From the pen of a young actor stepping from the 'family' of a long-running West End musical to the film factory that was Pinewood, his experiences of mid-20th century theatre and film-making are interwoven with a romance that came to the desert film location – literally – on wings of fire. A youthful romance which followed him back to London and is the theme of this memoir.

Love, Life and Moving Pictures recalls what life was like for a boy-actor not only in the Libyan film-location but also in a London recovering from the war. A world of coffee houses, jazz clubs and the seamy gang-rivalry of Soho which pervaded London's theatre-land.

For the reader who wants to learn, or simply recall, what life was like growing up in a London where, before mobile phones, tuppence in the pocket and a red phone box was the essential communication tool. A world where the solitary one-channel TV gave the viewer great plays, performed on Sunday and repeated live on Wednesday (Ampex recording was still several years away). A time before Anti-Social Behaviour Orders replaced flogging and when people who wantonly and pitilessly killed would themselves stand in peril of the same fate.

This was a world soon to be as alien as the jerky monochrome images of the Edwardian horse-bus and suffragettes of the previous generation. A serendipity look at a time captured here in forty-four thousand words as observed through youthful gaze of a teenage actor in the 1950s. Looking at a London recovering from a devastating war, its rising-generation casting off old values and with a thirst for adventure, romance and simply the rites of passage that is youth. A mid–twentieth century world met with youthful wide eyes intent on seeing all, before the state's long arm would reach out to swallow up two years – at eighteen surely an eternity? – in National Service.
A world before the Sixties assault on class and privilege.
A world vanished.
And cannot come again.

ಸಾಡ

Author

ಸಂಬಂ   Child-actor **TERENCE SHARKEY** was told by an understandably anxious leading-lady not to play with the apples on the table on the stage set for *The Enchanted Cottage*. "Just don't move. Sit very still and look like an angelic small boy" It was a long scene and the ten-years-old had not realised that his actions on the first night had not only distracted the audience but also driven the actress herself to distraction since she was trying to create a tender moment with her stage lover. The next night obediently he didn't move, he sat very still. Looking angelic was more difficult but he felt it had been reasonably achieved. Why then, the ten year old wondered, was she crying as the curtain fell?

He didn't have long to wait.

"You little bastard. You ate the apple!"

From there hopefully it could only be onwards and upwards – as the reader will see.

For Love, Life and Moving Pictures Terence has put aside his factual classic-crime writing pen, his industrial-training film writer's tools and has produced a tale of both the trials and tribulations of an African film-location and the ups and downs of a theatrical life in London seen through the eyes of a young stage and film actor in the changing times of mid 1950s London.

ಸಂಬಂ

Into my heart an air that kills
From yon far country blows:
What are those blue remembered hills,
What spires what farms are those?

That is the land of lost content,
I see it shining plain
The happy highways where I went
And cannot come again.

The Shropshire Lad
A.E. Housman. 1896

Chapter one

Audition

"Drop your trousers lad."

The request came in a dense Irish brogue.

"You said you can ride a camel, well that's going to show your legs."

Then as an afterthought, "Are you sure you can ride a camel?"

It was reasonable that my interrogator should question my assertion of five minutes earlier.

A thin small sixteen years old – going on twelve – I had by some standards done things outside the norm of many boys of my age but it had to be admitted (though I wasn't going to, not at this time) that opportunities for camel riding in post-war Camberwell were pretty thin on the ground. I gritted my teeth and loosened my grip on my trousers which fell obediently around my ankles. The panel of three men on the deep leather sofa looked impassively at my pale limbs and nodded approval. I had passed the visual test seemingly prerequisite to camel-riding and mercifully my thoughts, confused by the Irishman's curious request, gave no allowance for the likelihood of later discovery of my equestrian misrepresentation.

I was in the Irishman's house in Grosvenor Crescent Mews in London's fashionable Belgravia, in fact the large Georgian house belonged to the Duke of Westminster and the Irishman paid little rent, but I was not to discover that for many years. Nor too did I realise that I was in a house infamous in hedonistic circles for sudden unannounced, but nonetheless welcome, visits by guardsmen and their junior officers from the barracks of the nearby Brigade of Guards.

Brian Desmond Hurst, the Irishman, self-styled 'Empress of Ireland' whose life had begun in Belfast some sixty years before, was at the peak of his career and when not entertaining guardsmen would put his inimitable directorial stamp on motion pictures.

In pre-war Hollywood, the one-time set-designer had cut his teeth as assistant to the great John Ford. In 1928 he and John Wayne had appeared as extras in Ford's silent gothic-drama *Hangman's House*. It was soon apparent that Hurst was a powerful talent behind the camera where his painter skills captured faces and expressions with great artistry. He remained a lifelong friend of the Hollywood director, helping him years later in 1952 with Ford's film *The Quiet Man,* about an American (John Wayne) discovering his Irish roots. During the war Hurst had returned to England and in 1941 directed Anton Walbrook in the critically acclaimed *Dangerous Moonlight* (*Suicide Squadron-* *US*) and later earned a highly rated place in immediate post-war cinema with his critically acclaimed classics *Tom Brown's Schooldays* and *Scrooge. (A Christmas Carol-* US*)*

But all this was unknown to the skinny youth who stood with little dignity before the group, his trousers at half mast. As a child-actor well accustomed over some years to auditions, it had been the strangest of meetings. No cavernous theatre with anonymous silhouetted faces sitting in the mid-stalls darkness whose disembodied voices would give hope or disillusionment. These three; Brian the Director and two people I had no idea about whatsoever were within feet of me. And me Trouserless.

The director's stern face broke into a smile and he clapped his hands. "Time for a drink!" Then apparently surprised by the sight of this trouserless youth in his drawing room let out a roar. "Pull your pants up lad, you're making the place look untidy."

This was my introduction to J Arthur Rank's mighty organisation.

A week later I was standing beside the second of the men in the intimidating surroundings of Bow Street's Magistrates Court. The Court, whose dismal panelled walls had rung to the pleadings of Dr Crippen and his paramour Ethel le Neve fifty years before, now had (to me at any rate) no less an important task. The Children and Young Persons Act of 1933 had made it an offence to employ minors for the purpose of singing, playing, performing or being exhibited for profit, outside of Great Britain without a licence. It was the Court's task to ensure that a child's employer was a fit and proper person.

The severe figure on the Bench surveyed the little group. It was a strange band. The skinny youth (me), my mother and William MacQuitty the film's producer. Youth and mother were suitably overawed by the surroundings and said little. In answer to the magistrate's concerns regarding moral dangers, my mother (on the basis of one meeting with the producer over lunch) vouchsafed absolutely the rectitude of those to whom my morals would be entrusted. (I had carefully not mentioned to her the peculiar audition in Grosvenor Crescent Mews). Bill MacQuitty, an upright business man and family man with young children, whom I don't doubt had been discomforted by the audition, spoke convincingly of J.Arthur Rank's Methodism and recounted MacQuitty's own

Protestant boyhood in Belfast fifty years before. The Irish producer had worked with BDH over many years and within two years would produce *A Night To Remember,* still considered to be the definitive work on the maritime tragedy that was Titanic.

Twenty years before, in the thirties, film had been thought to lead people into bad ways. The *Methodist Times* complained about this, to which the *London Evening News* replied that the Methodist Church should look for a solution. Rank, the flour-miller stepped up to the challenge. Now he would feed not only the nation's stomachs but also their minds and souls. He founded the British National Films Company. By 1940, Rank owned five film studios, two newsreel companies and 650 cinemas. He dominated the British film industry and would continue to do so for the next 20 years. But one enterprise was nearest his heart. He established Religious Films Limited to make *Sunday Thoughts* to be shown on the Sabbath in every Odeon throughout the land. Hundreds of prints circulated each week but few reached the local screens whose managers feared the wrath of noisy audiences, where these devotional and virtuous contrasts were seen as an interruption to the Sunday entertainment.

The severe faced magistrate, suitably raised above we who stood before him in the body of the Court, took his task seriously. Like some mid-20th century Simon Cowell, his would be the yes or no that would say whether the thin youth would get the job. More precisely would the youth be at moral risk if a licence were to be issued to permit him to be employed abroad? The stern figure of Justice was minded, he said, to consider the matter in recess.

The court was opposite the fruit market. This was *My Fair Lady's* Covent Garden. A Covent Garden before the planners had sent the fruit porters packing and ponced-up the place for tourists. We found a market-porters' caff and sat around for half an hour or so amidst the myriad smells of overripe fruit and the warning cries of the fruit porters, loaded wicker-baskets ten or more balanced on their heads.

William MacQuitty, son of the Managing Director of the *Belfast Telegraph*, had spent fifteen of his fifty years, as a banker in the Far East with the Chartered Bank of India before returning to England to begin a tiny film production company, but this eminently respectable man-about-Pinewood who went on to produce such pictures as *"Above Us the Waves"* (*Secret Submarines* – US) and *"A Night to Remember"* would have had discreetly to edit bits of his curriculum vitæ from the gaze of the Justice of the Peace.

In his early twenties, broke and in Paris, he had acted as a runner on commission for Madame Estelle who ran the notorious bordello *House of all Nations* in Paris' deuxieme quarter. This was where King Edward VII had kept his famous love seat, expertly designed by a French carpenter to accommodate the regal portly frame while the monarch deftly pleasured simultaneously two or more of the ladies. Seek as diligently as I have, neither Ikea (nor the scarcely lamented MFI) seem ever to have matched this enterprising furniture.

MacQuitty's entrepreneurial bent had been simultaneously engaged with the Madame of another brothel which, whilst not enjoying the cachet of Royal Appointed knocking-shop, had a number of other attractions. *Le Piscine* – the Swimming Pool – a tableau-vivant where through a system of intricate mirrors its girls could be viewed as though the inquisitive client was prostrate at the bottom of a pool looking up at them walking on the surface. The pièce de résistance of this highly acclaimed pleasure-house was the *Crown of Queen Victoria* where the girls would sit in a circle facing inwards extending their arms towards the centre. The score or so of peach-like soft round derrières suctioned neatly to the glass above the guests' heads generally having prepared the viewers adequately for what might lie ahead, Madame would step in with the necessary pecuniary arrangements.

But these establishments where Kings could soak in baths of champagne with ladies, the more dextrous of whom could pick up coins off the edge of a table with their labias, were three decades and a world away from the business-suited producer and the austere Bow Street Court.

Of course none of this was known to the mother and boy who sat drinking mugs of coffee with the producer while in the court-room across the road my fate (for the next few months at any rate) was being decided. It was by no means easy to obtain these child-labour permits. It was summer 1955 and I had just left a two years engagement around the corner at Drury Lane which I had begun at fifteen. Fifteen was the minimum school-leaving age. Children in stage (and later film) performance, whether at home or abroad, had always rightly attracted the attention of the law-makers. The previous year the *Times* had quoted an outraged Bristol councillor who had opposed a licence for a twelve year old (the minimum age for stage performers) to dance in *The King and I* at Drury Lane. "After three months wild life in London the child would be totally unsettled. We have discouraged this precocity and these fanciful careers parents have for their children."

So the trio sat and waited nervously. William MacQuitty was nothing if not a positive man. He leaned forward, "Do you have a white suit Terence?" I shook my head dumbly. In Camberwell white suits were about as plentiful as camels. "Oh every young man should have a white suit, especially in Africa." I warmed to the word 'man', said softly in the producer's Belfast charm. It was the first time that day that any acknowledgement had been made to sixteen being hardly the 'child' envisaged in the eponymous Act of

Parliament. Yes, I liked that. I pictured myself white-suited, perhaps even in a fetching panama hat. That, thank God never came to pass.

The producer had arranged that the police constable guarding the vast doors of the Court would abandon his post and tell us when we were called. His portly frame appeared in the doorway of the caff.
"They're coming back Guvnor. You and the nipper will be wanted."
Back to earth, the self-image of the suave panama-hatted young man resumed the reality of the South-London boy in a dreadful herringbone suit. In both the eyes and parlance of the Law, 'a nipper'.

We made our way hastily over busy Bow Street. The great wall of the front of the Opera House casting its tall shadow over the grey court building as it had done for seventy years. *The Marriage of Figaro* was playing. Would the next few minutes bring Mozartian celebration or Wagnerian tragedy? (I can't honestly recollect that I was thinking all this at the time, but it's the kind of thing writers do years after an event - some readers even like it.)

With due ceremony the return of the stoney faced Justice of the Peace was proclaimed by the Clerk. As judges can, he took a while to get to the conclusion. No rapid Chaplinesque winning of the flower girl in one reel, no corpse in the swimming pool speaking in post-mortem voice-over to reveal the plot even before the opening-titles had ended. The J.P. consulted his notes, occasionally referring to an ancient leather-bound table of statutes and case-histories in child-labour. White-slavery that had seared itself into the pre-war minds of his and my mother's generation (assisted no-doubt by generous doses of opium-laden Anna May Wong movies) had not been forgotten. The Bench recited some cases where licences had been thwarted, the white blossom of youth assailed and a whole lot of nasty penalties had descended on the transgressing employer. A great moral responsibility would devolve onto the *Rank Organisation* and specifically Mr. William MacQuitty. Was he equal to the task?

The tall distinguished dark-haired Irishman rose to his feet. He took a moment to look around him and then with steady gaze affirmed and determined that the Court should be left with no doubt whatsoever that there was no better person in the land to be entrusted with this sacred undertaking.

The stony face above us broke into what passed for a smile.
"Then the Court will issue the licence, provisional for three months." He turned to me. "And a great adventure can begin for you young man."
I stood up, beaming that the Bench which had a moment earlier been referring to its duty to children, now acknowledged that whatever the nomenclature of the Law, the Justice could see before him a man. "Thank you Sir" I said. The smiling face leaned closer. "And mind you're a good boy for your mother."

The vision of the panama-hatted urbane sophisticate disappeared, never to return.

Outside the court in the July sunshine the producer turned to me. "Now for your white suit. Moss Bros is around here isn't it? At least that's what they say in their adverts. As it's your first, it's on the firm. I love adventures, don't you?"

Adventure?
I could never have dreamed.

ಸಿಂ

September 1955
The adventure begins

Chapter two

Location

The September night air in Tripoli is not much different from its hundred degree Fahrenheit day, cooler by a few degrees but with a humidity of almost a hundred percent three days out of four. In contrast to Heathrow's coolness eight hours earlier, the heat and stickiness hit the forty passengers as soon as the propellers stopped and the door of the BOAC Hermes was opened onto what served as Tripoli International Airport. The first thing that struck me was how dark it was, lit by oil lamps with a few electric bulbs whose original dimness was further obscured by layers of dust and sand and cobwebs. Though bearing the name of King Idris it was clear that royal patronage had not touched the place.

Cane tables and chairs, cigarette smoke spiralling into the slow swirling fans in the ceiling, everything a dirty white with bead-strung doorways and shabby waiters in red fez. On production of a BOAC plastic boarding card, both we who were alighting and the transits going on to Nigeria could get a soft drink in the fly-blown interior. The terminal building, if it could be called such, was straight out of *Casablanca*. Bogart's Rick Blaine was surely only a pace away, and wasn't that the shadow of Claude Rains' Captain Louis Renault keeping an eye on him? You must remember this?

Tripoli Idris International Airport 1955
Photo: Alan Tait

A shabby corrugated-iron hanger and the control tower were the only other buildings. The tower was small, square and white-painted with a few aerials and a radar dish on top. It was little bigger than a two-pump petrol-station back home and seemed unattended now that we had landed. There were no other aircraft to be seen. The Hermes had taxied right up to the apron outside the terminal-building and the passengers disgorged straight out in to the dingy bar or stood about on the terrace watching the primitive over-wing refuelling from drums by a sweating Arab at the semi-rotary pump.

This was 1955 and Libya was one of the poorest nations on earth, eighty percent of its population were nomads and its largest industry was from recycling of war-scrap from the equipment left in the desert by the allies and axis during the Second World War. Idris Airport was poorly equipped and served mainly as a staging post from Europe down to Nigeria, with a Royal Air Force detachment to service the strategic air corridor to East Africa and the Far East. The British had captured the Italian airfield during the war and renamed it RAF Castel Benito and in 1952 it had been named RAF Idris in honour of the king. In the night-time gloom it seemed to have no connection with the Jet age being born in the West. This was Tripoli's international airport.

The control tower and ancient hanger
Photo: Alan Tait

Arthur Alcott, Production Controller for Rank's Pinewood Studios was on hand together with Production Manager Teddy Joseph, I was in good hands. To a sixteen-years-old, sixty seems positively ancient but Arthur had been production controller at Gainsborough Studios in the 1940s and had gone on to oversee virtually all of Rank's Pinewood output since the end of the war. He appeared in the beaded alcove.

"Bit primitive here, but you'll like where we've put you."

And I did like it – a lot. We had sped the 21 miles through the darkness along the sand strewn road into the centre of the city where a dazzling palatial white-turreted building awaited. Tripoli's Grand Hotel as big as a royal palace had been serving visitors for seventy years. Arthur briefed over supper. I would take no part in the shooting during the coming week. Costumes, hair, make-up tests would be run and, as an afterthought and with a son of his own (John Alcott - later to win an Oscar with Kubrick) "We're all honorary members of the Beach Club so there'll be time to get to know everyone, just don't get burned."

Grand Hotel Tripoli 1955

The Grand overlooked the shimmering Mediterranean and was an enormous three-storied palace in white, surrounded by vivid green palms. At each corner was a square tower. In the centre front of this magnificent building another tower loomed, taller than the rest. Every one of the many windows was arched in Moorish style. In front, fountains played incessantly in the lush green gardens and in the centre of the drive was a cage with exotic animals.

The hotel had welcomed western guests over many years. It had stood unscathed through World War II. In 1941 it had watched Rommel march in with his Afrika Corps and then witnessed Monty and the British Eighth Army push him out again. All this had been a decade earlier, but all around could be seen the remnants of that time. I had seen the shanty towns on the way in from the airport, people living in houses made of army-tank fuel cans. In the evening at the bar, crew-members talked of the relics of tank-battles near the film-locations, these rusting memorials to the sad events and the lives lost, offering (for those who paused for thought) a curious reflection of the war-film we were now making

The unit had already been there a week and next morning would be shooting outside a café in the city centre. After breakfast I made my way there to meet the crew. Camels and carts were everywhere. Pitifully thin donkeys worked wearily as they had done for centuries among the crumbling white walls of the ancient city. The Phoenicians had settled here seven hundred years BC, then the Romans five hundred years later. Not much seemed to have changed. But it was not the strangeness of the surroundings that caught my eye. One thing dominated. The enormous camera. My film making experience in that year of the birth of Great Britain's commercial television age, when England's one television channel became two, was limited to making a few adverts in tiny London studios often with pre-war equipment. Generally this had been small, intimate gear and not all threatening. Here was something else. 200 AD met mid 20th Century technology head on. In front of the 2nd Century Arch of Marcus Aurelius, five men were perched around what appeared to be an enormous refrigerator which itself was mounted on a half-ton velocilator, pushed to facilitate tracking shots by three sweating men in khaki shorts.

By the mid 1950s the US film industry threatened by its nation's growing television had one mantra, Bigger, Better, Clearer and especially Colour. In the general haste, the old almost square cinema screen had been extended widthways. Most notably by *20th Century Fox* whose *Cinemascope* process had, in 1953, brought *The Robe* to appreciative audiences. *Cinemascope* involved taking the 35mm movie frame and squeezing almost double the picture-width on to it. The resulting tall elongated image was then unsqueezed in the local cinema.

Alone of all the major studios *Paramount* had rejected *Cinemascope* both for the distortions introduced by the lens and the quality-limitations of the necessary enlargement of the 35mm area when projected. *Paramount* had other ideas. Digging out a process abandoned in the late 1920s, they revamped the camera. A wider picture with no squeezing was achieved simply by widening the camera-aperture and turning the film sideways. The image was no longer placed width-wise constrained between the sprocket holes. Now it ran *along* the film and could, in theory be as wide as you liked. Thus, a negative with finer grain was created. The original jumbo-size print could simply be projected sideways as photographed, or alternatively, splendid standard release prints, grain-superior to *Cinemascope's* squeezed prints, were printed down to standard 35mm for local exhibition in widescreen.

The downside was that the transport-speed of the film through the camera was doubled, requiring bigger film spools for a given timing and the horizontal film movement required more space for the film-magazines. The increased speed meant increased noise, the camera was blimped like nothing I'd ever seen. Hence the 'refrigerator'. That sound-blimp size was 16 cubic feet (a domestic bath is a mere twelve). Additionally, film exposure required greatly increased light and power so this cinematic-dreadnought multiplied the accompanying arc-lamps and generators to supply them.

Thus in 1954, the previous year, was *Vistavision* born. In the United States *MGM, United Artists* and *Universal* embraced it. In Great Britain it would be widely used by *Rank*, the principal producer for the next decade.

Nowadays, any afternoon or wee small hours television-viewer watching endless re-runs of 1950s output will be aware that mid-twentieth century cinema audiences craved war pictures. Whether big Hollywood spectacle or the more compact, British stiff upper-lip stuff, they couldn't get enough. MacQuitty had just produced a gritty sea drama *Above us the Waves*, (*Secret Submarines-US*) now he was looking to the desert war.

World War II. A wounded army-captain is nursed in the nomadic Bedouin tents by the daughter of the Sheik. They marry. El Alemein beckons and the captain is killed rescuing another. His child is born. A decade later his brother discovers the truth and goes in search of the boy, the heir to the captain's estate and a new life in England. The boy must choose.

For this move to dry land two of Rank's leading British film actors had been lined up. Anthony Steel would play the army officer. Bringing to the role his wartime experience with the Grenadier Guards and later operational jumps with the paratroopers'. Steel was Pinewood's highest paid actor (along with Dirk Bogarde). Since joining Rank's charm-school in 1948 he'd had many matinée-idol roles coming to prominence in 1950 in the escape film

The Wooden Horse. Blue eyed, clean-jawed, square-cut. His was the definitive face of the hero.

Donald Sinden was the brother seeking news a decade later. The actor had spent the last year of the war with the Entertainments National Service Association (ENSA) touring liberated Europe and India. In 1953 he had begun a seven-year contract with the *Rank Organisation* and enjoyed enormous popularity from roles as diverse as comedy *Doctor* films to the gritty realism of *The Cruel Sea*. Earlier in 1955 he had made *Above us the Waves* which MacQuitty had produced.

Brian Desmond Hurst would direct. He had worked earlier with both stars. In 1953 he'd directed Anthony Steel in *The Malta Story* and this year he had directed the Kenyan Mau-Mau chronicle *Simba* with Donald Sinden as the local police chief. Hurst and MacQuitty went back a long way. The producer had cut his film-making teeth as assistant to Hurst on the British government's Crown Film Unit's *Letter from Ulster* in 1942. A quarter of a million U.S. troops were based in Northern Ireland and the Ministry of Information was keen to defuse tensions between them and the local population. During the shooting of the film MacQuitty never failed to be surprised at the film-union restrictions about who should touch what. Over-equipped and over-manned for a simple film, his impatience with the delays of such internal restrictions never left him and were to be a source of irritation – and Irish ingenuity – during the Tripoli experience to come. In 1944 came another opportunity for the two. Sidney Box had started *Verity Films* and was producing *On Approval* with Clive Brook and Bea Lilley to be shot at Denham, Europe's largest studio. BDH was engaged to direct and took Bill along as assistant.

In the event BDH was eventually fired and the credits show Brook as Director. Inauspicious though this second coupling was for their professional teamwork, MacQuitty and BDH remained close friends. Now ten years later, (as Brian had prophesied at the time) the producer-director partnership was reactivated.

The promise of a week to acclimatise to the suffocating heat never materialised. Two days after arriving I made the two-hour journey into the desert, its sand-blown tarmac being for most of the time the only salient feature. The location was at a small oasis in the vast expanse of rolling yellow Sahara where the set-builders had erected a long line of berber-blanketed black tents, before which the action would take place.

All I was required to do that day was to run from a tent where my uncle had discovered me, circumnavigate some grazing sheep and goats and disappear into a foreground tent. Simple enough. But children and animals…..
I was leaving nothing to chance and I did a few dummy runs. The goats, fiercely armed with horns continued to eat placidly as I sped by. Not so the sheep. The sheep were not going to co-operate. Their scattering was visually effective but threatened to cast me into the slippery excrement that lay all around and made running difficult and dangerous. Carefully I worked out where my feet could land without slipping. I noticed that a few sheep were tethered and as these were avoided by the scatterers, their proximity gave me safe passage beside them.

It was to be taken in one shot. The boy would run from the tent, chased by the uncle, towards the camera. BDH slid out of his deck-chair.
"Come with me" he growled.
We walked in silence to the distant end of the long shot. It was a long walk and an uncomfortable silence. I broke it amiably.

"I worked out where I can run so the sheep won't trip me."
The Director stopped and looked at me witheringly.
"You'll do as you're told!"
The Irish bark was fierce. I was astonished. In theatre the director invariably welcomed the participation and contribution of the actor, who oftentimes would see a workaround for some entrance or some business with a prop. This was my first taste of the receiving end of absolute power. (I learned later that this was a quite usual opening gambit for BDH with his actors and he is on record as recommending it to all budding directors.)
Well now he'd told me, so now I knew.

Donald Sinden was inside the distant tent. He grinned encouragingly and made some remark about the sheep shit. This recollection about one of British theatre's most distinguished knights is coloured with the sound even after all these years, *that bassoon-like mellifluous voice intoned "sheep-shit" as though the syllables were wrought by Shakespeare himself.*

Terrified of the wrath of the director if I messed up, I trembled as the necessary procedures for even this simple scene were carried out. Light-readings were taken, camera gate was checked for hairs, the tape measure was carefully rolled out for focus, the markers were placed in the sand for the actors' positioning and arc-lights were brought up to their full glare competing with the deep shadows from the brilliant sun. And like pulling a tooth it was all over in an instant. One take. The Director came over and patted my head.
"You see, the sheep took care of themselves, the sheep were alright."

As I got to know the man, I came to realise that his bark was far worse than his bite. He was possibly a kindly man at heart but his style of leadership and perhaps a personal loneliness gave him this bluster that probably repelled many. I had been warned about the acerbic director. It was well known that on the set of *On Approval* ten years before, his directness had got him into trouble. All were tired. There had been a long and complicated scene-dressing and an intricate lighting and effects rehearsal. The camera had just started turning. Wearily the director called "Action". From his position on the set Clive Brook suddenly turned to the Director, "Brian this is my wrong side. I'll have to come in from the other side and exit left."

BDH surveyed the scene slowly and carefully and in measured tone said quietly in his high-pitched Irish brogue, "Go and fuck yourself."

Brian Desmond Hurst
His painter skills captured faces and
expressions with great artistry.

The veteran star had walked out of the stunned studio. In the event it turned out that his face had been injured as a pilot during the First World War, Brook had not mentioned it and probably BDH, himself a battle survivor from Gallipoli, was sorry later. But it was a mark of the man that his directness could equally be aimed at his master (Clive Brook was financing the production) as well as his servant, the small actor.

We lunched in the shade of the tents; ham, eggs and chips apparently being the favourite, location-catering having avoided the cous-cous and sheep's brains beloved of the Bedouin. The exposed Technicolor had to be kept cool in giant Thermos flasks and was to be returned to a brewery's cold-room in Tripoli to await flight to London for processing. I hitched a lift in the despatch-car after lunch. The desert miles back did little to enamour the scenery to me. Its sand which permeated everything seemed just slightly less abrasive than the Director.

༶

A bunch of magicians in the Sahara.
Chief sorcerers
BDH and Bill MacQuitty seated centre
Crew *The Black Tent*. October 1955

Chapter three

Grand Hotel

Grand Hotel breakfast was a great and decorated affair. At the end of the cavernous dining room a vast oak table resembling an altar was piled high with every imaginable fruit that Africa could provide. The usual cereals were there and enormous pottery flagons of juices. Behind it all was the high priest in tall chef's hat conjuring up in an instant, concoctions of eggs, bacon and it seemed absolutely anything requested of him. I was late down to breakfast, the queue that had usually formed in my first days was long gone and I was in line behind a solitary young girl, about seventeen I supposed who, wrestling with a bandaged arm was not making much progress. She was in an hotel bathrobe, her golden hair tied up with bright red ribbon.

"You've been in the wars," I said. "Can I reach things?"
She nodded without smiling and I poured out the juice and selected some fruit. She nodded approval. I ordered eggs and bacon for us from the high priest. She followed me to my table and sat without speaking.
I made small talk. When had she arrived? Why was she here? But she just stared blankly with great sad eyes that scarcely moved from the table cloth. I asked if she was alright. She nodded.
The silence hung. When will she say something more I wondered. When I returned from getting the eggs she had gone. Later that morning one of the unit secretaries with the call sheet for the next day found me. Had I heard the awful news?

The Argonaut had refuelled in Rome, ready for its long haul across the night Sahara, just a short touch-down in Tripoli and then on to Kano and Lagos. The Mediterranean skies were already darkening as the aircraft lifted off from Ciampino. Today the Argonaut was full. Margaret Denys-Burton, in a team of three busied herself with clearing dinner for the forty passengers. These were the days of one class, china plates and silver-service. Cocktails had preceded the six-course dinner and the three cabin-crew were kept busy in the three-hour leg from Rome to Tripoli. Some passengers relaxed in the cocktail bar and now Margaret went back to ask them to return to their seats for the landing at Idris Airport.

On the flight deck Captain R.D.E Griffiths and First Officer Davies, experienced World War II flyers, both with the airline for nine years. They, together with the navigation officer and radio officer made up the standard crew of seven. None of the crew had flown together but all had done the trip several times before. Out from Heathrow on the twenty-one hour journey to Nigeria. With refuelling stops at Rome and Tripoli and across the Sahara to Kano then Lagos on Africa's west coast. Today's trip was shorter, for the crew had joined the aircraft in Rome.

Tripoli air controllers made contact and the aircraft descended as Griffiths smoothed the four Merlins into the final approach. The thirty-nine years old ex-Royal Australian Air Force pilot had attained his mastery of four-engine flying on the Sunderland flying-boat bombers of Coastal Command and had joined BOAC on demob. His promotion from first officer in 1946 to Argonaut Captain in March 1954 had been steady. An experienced captain, he had almost 10,000 hours on his log, reflected in his £1600 a year salary. He peered into the gloom, BOAC had a minimum 1000 yards for night landings at Idris and the Australian was reassured by at least 1600 yards visibility. There was no low cloud and he began a visual approach to runway 11.

He preferred the longer runway 18, but tonight the effects of the sirocco, the desert winds known as *ghibli* justified the shorter landing to minimise cross-wind effects. Runway 18 was equipped with better approach aids; namely lead-in lights, a locator beacon and the VHF Direction-Finding more favourably positioned to ease an aircraft landing. He was fully aware that the lighting to runway 11 was less adequate. Although equipped with an electric flare path with four sodium lights at each end there was no lead-in or approach illumination. Auxiliary gooseneck lighting had been lit, but these primitive paraffin flares that marked the runaway were of little help. The attempt was aborted as the wind took over and the aircraft overshot the runaway. Griffiths circled, approached and lined up the aircraft a second and third time. After the second overshoot the Approach Controller radioed that he would assist the lining up by sending someone with a Very-light pistol to the threshold of runway 11 as the aircraft made the final approach.

In the cabin Margaret could see that some of the passengers had noticed that the aircraft had been circling the airport for almost twenty minutes and three times had swooped down on the airfield only to climb again. She smiled reassuringly. It was unusual but she knew that Captain Griffiths had landed here a dozen times before, always at night. Beside her, steward William Gouldie busied himself with the landing procedures. Training just completed this was only his second flight, tomorrow he'd be thirty-one and was looking forward to celebrations Lagos-style. His colleague Charles Smart too was smiling reassuringly at the passengers as the three cabin staff prepared for landing.

First Officer Jim Davies had known a few other anxious times, you couldn't avoid it in 7000 hours flying and he knew what to do. In the dimmed red lighting of the flight deck the glowing ultra-violet of the altimeter held his attention. He reminded the Captain that it had been set to a QNH setting showing height above sea level rather than a QFE setting showing height above the airfield. The Captain, scrutinising the darkness below, replied he was aware. A fourth approach. Davies called "Runway ahead." Griffiths too could see the lights of the runway and decided to make a visual approach. A slight turn to port and the runway was dead ahead. The altimeter he noted was showing 610 feet, about 350 feet above runway level.

He was not at all apprehensive about continuing to attempt to land on runway 11. His only difficulty was lining up with the runway in the wind and worsening visibility. He calculated that he could still spend a further 30 minutes over the airfield without encroaching on the fuel reserve necessary for diversion to his alternative airport at Malta. The Met forecast earlier had anticipated visibility at Idris to be 16 km possibly decreasing to 6 km in 'suspended sand'. In reality Griffiths was faced with less than two kilometres and little in the way of approach lighting.

The turbulent conditions were making accurate flying difficult and the aircraft pitched and yawed. The runway lights gave insufficient clues as to attitude, height and angle of approach. Below, Griffiths could see the amber and blue lights of the perimeter track and ahead the receding V of semi-recessed white lights and oil flares that marked the runway. Within a few seconds of beginning the fourth visual approach the Captain had lost sight of the lights in a cloud of billowing sand, he reverted to instrument flying but it was too late.

Davies saw the trees first, "Look out! Climb!"

Griffiths pulled back on the throttles but at that moment with a shuddering and sickening tearing sound the Argonaut's silver underbelly ripped through the tops of the tall eucalyptus trees. The aircraft dipped and ploughed its way into the sand of the olive grove, swerving over to jam the port exit doors. The four propellers tore into the desert, spraying sand in their wake. In the darkness red tongues of flame licked at the silver fuselage. The wings had broken off and lay beside the aircraft, spewing fuel from their ruptured tanks. Within moments the whole aircraft was ablaze. It was just 400 yards short of the runway.

I found her in the lounge. At the far end of the cavernous marble hall, lost in an enormous settee but still instantly recognisable by the bright red hair ribbon. She caught my gaze and beckoned. A gleaming tray upon which the hotel's impeccable silver was catching the afternoon sunlight sat before her on the low table. "Would you like some tea?" I nodded and sat down.

"I was rude this morning," she said. The averted gaze of breakfast no longer.

"Of course not."

"Yes I was, I left you with my breakfast."

"It didn't matter. I ate it, I was hungry – and anyway it was I who was rude. I said something to you about you being in the wars. You understand, I didn't know what had happened, I wouldn't have joked."

"I knew that, thank you. I suppose I just felt so lost and foreign here. And in a dressing gown!"

I looked at her, her clothes had changed. The fullest soft blue silk skirt trembled in the breeze from the ceiling fans and I was aware of the undulating white silk blouse as she breathed.
She caught my gaze." You're with the film people aren't you?"
I nodded. "You know about us?"
"One of your costume ladies had spotted my hotel robe at breakfast and made these things for me. She just knocked on my door and said she'd heard I hadn't got any clothes. I cried, it was so kind. Everyone's been so kind." Her blue eyes filled with tears.
"Are you alone, have you someone here?"
"They took Mummy with the others to the RAF sick quarters and then on to the Military Hospital. I suppose we were lucky. They say a lot were...."
Her words faltered, she bit her lip, refusing to acknowledge.
I obliged. "Fifteen they say, and many badly injured!"
It was infamously clumsy. One of those moments when you want the floor to open, one of those moments of crassness you remember all life long.
She shuddered. "I don't want to talk about it - if you don't mind."
English politeness carrying the mood.
I sat silently foot in mouth.
She broke the moment. "What do you do? With the film I mean."
"I'm an actor."
"Is it hard out there, working in all that heat?"
Well I haven't done much. I was out there yesterday. Just me and some sheep."
I could have added "Oh, and one of the biggest stars in Rank's firmament," but somehow that seemed excessive and misplaced. For now the sheep would suffice.
"It was my first day. All a bit strange."
"How did it go?"
"Well the Director said the sheep were good."
Silence descended again. Not one of the comfortable intimate silences when people know each other but one of those jagged

pauses where the mind desperately seeks continuity. Rescue came in the form of a red-fezzed waiter with another pot of tea and a plate piled high with cream cakes. She remarked about the flies which buzzed and pitched and challenged relentlessly for the food.

I nodded. "It's worse out at the location. They're everywhere. We're all under absolute instructions to keep washing our hands. But apparently loads are getting Tripoli Trot."

Her tightly bandaged arm reminded me that this dire warning of things lavatorial must pale into insignificance beside the carnage she had endured in the blazing Argonaut the night before and again I felt rather silly. Sixteen years old I decided, did not prepare for some conversations. And I didn't even have that excuse any more, I had turned seventeen the day before flying out.

She nodded politely. "How long have you been here? You're not very brown."

"I arrived on Sunday."

"Oh God! Three days! You could have been booked on the same plane....."

Her voice tailed off. Desperately I looked for a way out. "Look, would you like to come out to Sabratha tomorrow?"

"What's that?"

"It's a Roman ruin. A big amphitheatre place. The unit's out there."

"I'd like that."

We finished our cakes without the conversation sagging or revisiting the events of the darkened airfield of the night before. She stood up, I rose and formally she shook my hand.

"Will you be down for dinner?" I asked.

"Yes. I'll look out for you."

And she was gone.

The ancient ruin that is Sabratha lies some 40 miles to the west of Tripoli on the Mediterranean coast and is a gateway to the Sahara. Great columns of sandstone that have endured the centuries since 500 BC surround the late 3rd Century ancient stage. Stone galleries form the seating, rising in a sweeping semi-circle before the stage below. Behind the stage is a great three-storey architectural backdrop of columns and windows and galleries which run like a maze. All magnificently set in front of the turquoise Mediterranean.

Arranging the trip had not been without difficulty. The production office had at first not viewed it kindly. Visitors to the location were discouraged to the point that even the producer's young wife Betty was banned. But I had an ally. A passing crew-member simplified it to the stoney faced secretary.
"Look Glad, this is an extreme case. The young lady has just survived a nightmare we could all have been in if they'd booked us to fly later. Terry's just trying to take her mind off it. You've said there's a space in the crew-bus. Come on where's your heart?"
Thus assailed the place in the vehicle was assigned. Bert my ally winked at me. "She seems nice that young lady. And she likes talking to you, I could see at your table tonight, I think you're good for her, you look good together."
Foolishly, I felt the colour rising in my cheeks. "It's nothing like that. I just feel I want to help."
His gaze fixed mine."Oh yeah?" A scarcely perceptible shake of the head. "See you in the morning."

Rosemarie and I had climbed up into the sandstone corridors that formed the backdrop to the stage. From somewhere she had borrowed shorts which showed off the longest smoothest limbs I had ever seen. At Drury Lane the chorus were famed for their appearance and I suppose that I fancied myself as something of a connoisseur. I had never seen legs that seemed to go on for ever, except in the pin-up of Cyd Charisse on the dressing room wall. All around the blue sky made stark contrast to the vivid yellow sand. The midday sun was scorching the ancient stone and making it difficult to touch. Below us, two actors Anton Differing and Frederick Jaeger were playing out a scene in which as part of

Rommel's Afrika Korps they are enjoying a bit of sight-seeing. One was photographing the other. We could hear the guttural German. "Eines zwei drei. Alles ist klar."

"Will they subtitle that?" We were anxious not to be noticed and Rosemarie whispered as we peered down to the amphitheatre.

"No I think the idea is that it's simple German conversation, easily understood and is more realistic if they leave it that way."

Sabratha 500BC The stage was added in the third century.
Its setting beyond any Broadway designer's dream.

Suddenly the quiet scene below was rent with a mighty roar and a jet aircraft screamed low across the open sky. Rosemarie gave a cry of terror and clung to me, trembling and sobbing. I could feel her heart pounding and her breasts pressing into my chest.

"Rosemarie, it's nothing. It's the Americans. They've got a base, Wheelus Field, the other side of the city. They fly over the location to see what we're doing. It's just a nuisance, but nothing to be worried about."

She stayed clinging to me for some minutes giving little sobs, then drew away. It was hard not to notice beneath her blouse her nipples straining against the smooth white silk. Trembling, she took my handkerchief and dabbed at her eyes.

"Such a noise, it reminded me….It was all noise. And no one could move. The door on my side had jammed against the sand and I couldn't open it. Then the steward got us to the door on the other side but an African chief's robes got caught. Oh it was horrible. There was an old lady strapped in and people trampling over her and the floor had come up and the seats had collapsed and people's legs were trapped. And the flames. Oh God the flames."

Her body racked with sobs and again she held me tightly, her nails biting into my shoulders. Then, suddenly aware of our proximity she drew away, letting go of me and blushing. "I'm sorry. That jet, it just brought it all back."

I took both her hands in mine. "It's understandable. It's going to be like that for a long time I think."

Down below us the unit was breaking for lunch and we made our way down to where tables had been set up on the black and white mosaic and where over centuries Roman Legionaires, Byzantian Centurions, German Generals and British Field Marshalls had assuaged their appetites and where now we who played at war would do the same. A white bell tent had been erected for the catering. Bert was leaning on the heavily-laden table. He looked over to where Rosemarie was sitting.

"Does she like Sabratha?"

"A lot. It took her mind off Wednesday night."

"You didn't upset her did you? She looked as though she's been crying."

"It was that jet. It startled her and sort of brought it all back. It's not forty-eight hours yet."

"That's the Yanks. Bloody nuisance. They like to see what's going on, although what they can see at a thousand miles an hour or

34

whatever they do is beyond me. Crazy flyers. I was with them in Cambridge in the war. They was good though. Did the daylight raids over Germany. God, it was bad enough in the dark and I did enough of them. But them Yanks had some nerve. And plenty never got back."

It seemed as though war sacrifice was never far from peoples' minds. Though finished ten years before, somehow the littered remnants in the desert, or just the proximity of where so many grim battles had been fought, seemed to make everyone more conscious.

Bert piled a third egg on his plate. "Well she's enjoying lunch now. Poor kid, I saw that mess at the airport, not much left, not with the fire and all. An RAF bloke told me there was 600 gallons of fuel went up. The plane just melted, great pools of aluminium in the sand. I keep thinking how any of us could have been on it."
He paused and reached into the pocket of his shorts.
"Here I looked these out for you."
He slapped a narrow violet coloured envelope on to the table. Inside I could see three neat square paper packets.
He misread my puzzled look.
"Johnies. Durex. You know."
"Bert! It's not like that. I only met her yesterday."
Rosemarie was approaching. Panic stricken I seized the envelope from the table.
Bert grinned. "Just look after her. I've got two girls, Lord help the bugger that gets any of mine into trouble. Oh and I'd stop waving them about if I was you, it's not very subtle like."

.....

The knock was soft but insistent. I had turned in early after dinner, room-service had brought tea and I lay in bed reading the script. She stood in the doorway. "Oh, you're busy."

I put down the script. "No, what's up?"

"There are cockroaches in my room."

"They're in everybody's room. The Waddan Hotel is full of them too so the crew tell me."

"What shall I do? They're enormous and make that scrabbling noise all the time."

"Well I tried stepping on one. It exploded like a ripe plum."

She recoiled at the theatrical description.

I tried to be more helpful. "I put a towel in the waste paper bin and stick them in there, it keeps them quiet.

"The best hotel in town and it has roaches!" She grimaced at the contents of the bin.

"Well Cleopatra used to wear them, they're sacred or something. But I don't care to think of the kitchens here. Anyway I have a theory. if you can't do anything about it, just live with it. You sort of get used to them in old theatres back home, even though they're not as big there – or scrabblier."

Her blue eyes widened. "Scrabblier! There's no such word!" We laughed and agreed that there was no point in resisting the insistent creatures.

It was the first time I had heard her laugh, light and tinkling like a bell. She had certainly had nothing to laugh about in the last couple of days.

I looked in the teapot."Would you like a drink?"

There was only one cup and she went into the bathroom and returned with a glass.

"Won't it crack?" I asked.

"I don't think so. They drink mint tea out of glasses, it seems to be something they like to do when you go in a shop."

The tea was poured and she sat beside me on the bed.

"Have you a lot to learn?" Her long fingers caressed the script.

"No, did it all in England, there's not that much anyway. And most of it will be back at Pinewood before Christmas, so I've plenty of time."

"Is it difficult? Remembering all that?" She asked politely.
"Well I'm a bit out of practise, I've been in a play for a couple of years so it all became a bit automatic. But you don't forget. You just read with a card covering the cues, to test your memory."
"Would you read some for me?" she propped herself up against the pillow
"Well you could be on the book for me."
Her blue eyes quizzed me, puzzled by the jargon.
"I mean give me my cues."

Her voice as she read the uncle role was light and she laughed at my different interpretations. It seemed that the simple task at least took her mind off the events of two nights before. I excused myself and went into the bathroom.

When I returned she was asleep. What to do now? Slumbering on my bed clad only (my fertile imagination supposed) in the hotel bath robe was a young woman I had known for barely 36 hours. I remembered her body clinging to me long after the jet had screamed over and it all seemed very natural. The night heat, scarcely assailed by the slowly revolving ceiling fan, was the only cover we needed. I leaned over, she had a different expression for the sad tenseness that had surrounded her in the day had gone, her soft skin relaxed. I turned off the light and she sighed softly as I cradled her in my arms. It all seemed very natural.

ಸಂಙ

Chapter four

Having a ball

When I awoke she was gone. At breakfast she apologised for wearing the same skirt and blouse and I suggested we go sightseeing and to the *souk* to shop. I had ordered a *gharry* and the horse-drawn carriage was drawn up in front of the hotel, its Libyan-driver shod in sandals and the usual baggy white pants that Arabs wore. A white vest trimmed ornately with gold braid and on his head a close fitting cotton cap in vivid burgundy completed the outfit. Rosemarie sat beside me as the horse accelerated through the huge black gates on to the Lungomare Boulevard between the hotel and the sea. Libya had been an Italian colony until WW2 and Mussolini had done his best to develop Tripoli as a holiday resort. The Italian Cathedral lay a few streets away, it looked as if it had been lifted straight from Rome. The waterfront was beautifully laid out with gardens and avenues of palms and flowering trees and fountains. Everywhere Tripoli gleamed white, mosques and minarets passed by, their golden adornments catching the sun.

A typical gharry

Ahead of us at the harbour lay the ancient Barbary Fort which marked the the old city boundary. As forts should be, the only windows were high in its flat white impregnable front. Cannon projected through the arched windows on the tall tower, with battlements above. And all around the ubiquitous green palm trees. Errol Flynn, Lawrence of Arabia, take your pick. These same cannon had fired on the US Marines during the Barbary Coast pirate-war at the start of the 19th century, giving rise to the words of the Marine Hymm "…..*to the shores of Tripoli.*"

We soon tired of the museum, a few rooms displaying rusty relics of the pirates. The gharry made its way through an archway of the fort that led into the old city. Into the cramped *souk*, between the shabby crumbling buildings teeming with people. Mounds of coloured spices vied with bales of cloth and trinket sellers crowded the carriage. Rosemarie took my arm,
"Lets walk."

Barbary Fort, Tripoli
Little changed from 1803 when the prisoners from the captured frigate USS Philadelphia were kept in the dungeons. Its ramparts were the platform for Mussolini and later Ghadaffi. Controlled by Italy since 1911, Libya fell to the Allies in 1943 and remained under British control until independence in 1951.

I demurred. We would be crushed under the mass, but she insisted and we climbed down into the dust. It was clear that the Arab sellers were fascinated by our blondeness. Especially that of the young woman on my arm.

The Arab women in public were wearing the traditional barracan, white woollen pulled over their head and revealing generally just one eye. Shrouded from head to toe only bare feet or sandals could be glimpsed. Libyan culture at that time was locked back many centuries and women were still covered, shapeless and invisible, treated more as property than people. In contrast, Rosemarie shone like a beacon, red ribbon in blonde hair brushed to a glow. Her blouse accentuating her thrusting breasts over narrow waist. That and sleek legs and shapely feet in gold sandals challenged every male eye.

Many of the men were dressed like our driver But the more traditional kept to the ancient roughly textured barracan in brown or white worn over a light cloth around their head and shoulders and descending to their knees, where the whole ensemble finished with very baggy trousers and dusty sandals. Years later I was contesting the Slough parliamentary seat and got to know and like many Moslems and learned that these trousers or *sirwal* were designed apparently so that the next holy Prophet may be born through the loins of a male. The very practicable baggy pants would ensure that the holy Prophet will not, upon birth, fall to the ground but be caught in the leggings of the pure white pants.

Eventually the sheer mass of sellers accompanying us through the *souk* proved overpowering, jostling and prodding, men touched my hair whose blondeness had been enhanced with a bit of unit hair-styllist Iris Tilley's magic the day before.
Rosemarie gave a shriek. "They keep touching me."
"Well we look different that's all. they're touching me too."
She gave me a fierce look. "Not where they're touching me!"
She held my hand tightly and we looked around for the driver as he hastened the cab towards us.

The Underwater Fishermen of Tripoli had organised a ball for that evening in the hotel ballroom and our star, a young Italian actress playing my mother, would be presenting prizes. Considering the major role she had as Steel's co-star, Anna Maria Sandri's English was virtually non-existent. Despite the language barrier she was charming and was well-liked by everybody. The unit would be going in support. She was fluent in French and we had conducted a very stilted introduction, scarcely assisted by my schoolboy *Franglaise*. There was to be another celebration. Producer Bill MacQuitty and a Libyan policeman had earlier that week scuba-dived in the harbour for a WW2 unexploded shell and had removed it to deeper, safer water.

I had come down early to the ball and the band was still setting up as Rosemarie appeared. At the top of the grand marble staircase she paused and looked around. She spotted me and waved and I waited on the bottom step as she glided down towards me. Her entrance had not escaped the Arab drummer who struck a drum roll down every step to a great crash of cymbals at the bottom. She blushed delightedly.

"Do you think he always does that?"

"That's nothing" I said. "Wait till you leave!"

"Then I'm not going. Everyone is looking."

And everyone *was* looking.

She caught my gaze and struck a pose. "Alice again, she is so kind. Apparently these bracelets are for some wedding scene in the picture – but I get to wear to them first!"

Wardrobe, in the form of Alice, had worked its generous magic again. A halter neck of gold lamé crossed the top of an intense white full length slim-fitting silk gown where it began, scarcely concealing her bosom. The silken sheen followed her body, over curving hips to where it descended to the floor. Around her slim waist a wide gold lamé belt draped to where a low frontal strategic knot drew the eye as it fell as a wide glistening tie to her knees. Fastened to the back like some butterfly wings, two silk pieces in iridescent blue served to cover her bandaged arm and were clipped to a gold bracelet at each wrist, fluttering and shimmering as she walked. The ensemble needed no traditional gilded Cleopatra headdress. Rosemarie's golden hair tumbled around her neck and a neat black rope wound into the curls crowned the vision. The gold glinted on her slim wrists and her perfume assailed my nostrils. She was quite simply, stunning.

No one should have been surprised. Beatrice Dawson, was an ace film-costume designer and had credits going back to the forties. Hers had been the deft eye in Deborah Kerr's *Black Narcissus* wardrobe and the *Caesar and Cleopatra* costuming for Vivienne Leigh and Stewart Granger. She headed an expert and talented team for our Wardrobe in Tripoli. The sheer artistry of what could be achieved with a moment's sketching and a few nimble stitches was breathtaking. The following year Beatrice would design for Marilyn Monroe in *The Prince and the Showgirl*. Dietry problems meant that the goddess' figure went up and down and facsimile dresses were made to accommodate. "I had two ulcers on that film – both monogrammed MM" she said. Tonight her team's creation on Rosemarie's hour-glass frame turned every head.

The evening swept by. The 1950s saw Arabic music influenced by the West and the air was full of familiar dance music, but still redolent of the East with tarabaki drums, piccolo and cymbals a constant reminder of Tripoli's world around us. Robed Arab sheiks in square cloth chequered headdresses bound with gold rope gyrated beside Rosemarie, giving an odd authenticity to her Queen of the Nile appearance, the whole totally enchanting. The Libyan music was augmented by a hill-billy band from the U.S. base at Wheelus Field and the appearance at one point of a bejewelled Eastern belly-dancer undulating to *I Want to be a Cowboy's Sweetheart* was an unforgettable mark of east meeting west.

Rosemarie tried not to show it, but despite all the gaiety around she still had, in unguarded moments, that haunted look that I had seen that first morning two days before. Her mother was recovering in the military hospital where she visited each day and still Rosemarie avoided any talk of the crash. By ten o'clock she made her excuses and I escorted her up the marble stairway.

We reached the corridor to her room. Rosemarie took my hand and drowned me in her enormous blue eyes. "Will you be my Night?"
"What?" I could hear my heart thumping. Had I misheard?
I had.

"I said 'Will you be my knight'- you know the shining armour bit – with the cockroaches. I put the waste-bin out but I can't bear picking them up, and they run so."

We went into her room. As the lights went on, the creatures scampered for the walls or any shadow that was available. Rosemarie gave a shriek. These were like no local theatre or palace-of-varieties beatles back home. The Empire certainly hadn't set on these gigantiques. The dull brown creatures were all about two inches long, as big as my thumb and when not dashing for cover would climb walls with antennae waving and even fly a short distance. It was a losing battle and having captured a dozen or so we gave up. She went to the bathroom door.
"Would you mind if I shower? It was so hot down there and that dance I was doing with the American is definitely not suited to this part of the world".
I sat on the bed. "I think he called it jitterbug. But you certainly seemed to keep up. I wish I could dance."
Having few terpsichorean skills I had had to content myself with sitting at the bar while she danced, but she had seemed as pleased to sit out with me, sipping soft drinks and talking about everything and nothing. Her father was in the new oil fields in the Niger Delta in Nigeria. Oil had been discovered there the previous year and the Dutch company for whom he worked was expanding through the forests. She was at boarding school in England and had been going out to see her father when the crash occurred. She had disappeared into the bathroom and I could hear the shower running.

A few minutes later and she was framed in the doorway. Her bath robe was on the bed and she had dressed again in the sheer white silk dress which clung to every curve of her damp body. She had taken off the hooped earings and the gold bangles and only the necklace remained. She came into the room and went to the table where a jug sat on a silver tray. "Would you like some orange?"

As she poured, the light from the ornate table lamp behind her bathed her in its amber glow, filtering through the diaphanous material.

The necklace was still wet. It had defied her pre-shower attempt to remove it and now she looked to me. I rose and went to the table and she turned her back as my fingers found the catch. Her skin was smooth and cool and perhaps to my surprise I found I was deliberately trying not to touch her neck as I fumbled. It was as if the air was vibrant with electricity and that any contact would bring blue flashes.

The gold chain separated and she turned to me, her nipples pushing hard through the silk, I recalled how firm her breasts had felt against my chest in her terror at the ruins yesterday. I turned her face to the light, no words were spoken, as she leaned forward and we kissed. A long lingering gentle kiss. In an instant we had sunk onto her bed, the silken dress beside us on the floor, careless of the cockroaches. I felt her shiver. "You're not cold?"
"Of course not, I think it's what's called passion."
My lips brushed her neck beneath her blonde curls and she shivered again. I kissed the soft skin of her throat and a moment later she forced her breast into my mouth and moaned softly. We lay entwined, nerves tingling. Her fingers caressed and enticed. My tongue traced circles on the warm skin of her breasts and moved across her stomach down to her thighs. She moaned and presently my lips returned to hers. She coiled herself around me.
"Go on Terry, don't stop!"
"But I'm hurting you, I can feel it."
"Don't stop! I want you to. You do want to, don't you?"
Had the Pope ever been more Catholic?
A tender moment, made more so by the young woman gritting her teeth, determined it seemed both to enjoy and to share pleasure. A moment so exquisite yet so personal that even more than half a

century on I cannot bring myself to share. Some moments, just a few in life should perhaps have the seal of the confessional around them. This was such a one. It was her moment, our moment – and no one elses.

༺༻

Chapter five

Sincerity

The next morning the car left early. There was no dressing facility in the desert and everyone attended the unit production suite and left the hotel in a motley collection of army battledress, Bedouin robes and in my case as a distinctly odd blonde Arab in a sort of nightshirt. Donald Sinden, myself and other actors crushed together in the back of the Mercedes.

Donald Pleasance was playing the role of Ali, a wily Arab guide. He had been practising broken Italian with Anna-Maria at the ball last night and had discovered the musicality of the word *Sentimentali.* With an actor's love of words he practised it over much of the thirty miles to the location. How would Mussolini have said it on entering Abyssinia? How would Mario Lanza sing it? No sooner had the clever character-actor exhausted the variations than a crew member began singing some bawdy Sicilian ballad, learned on the Allies push through the region a dozen years before. The whole journey had taken on something of the noisy style of those seaside charabanc day trips so popular in the fifties.

Bert was already working when we arrived. He spotted me and hurried over.

"Well?" he grinned.

"Well what?"

"Did you do it?"

"Of course not" I felt the colour rising in my cheeks. He smiled, looked at me sideways and went on coiling a wire. Without turning he shook his head.

"That's not what your face is saying," he said drily. "Eddie's going to have his work cut out. (Eddie Knight – Make-up artist.) Desmond's lit you for a brown-skin not a redskin. Don't worry, I'll have a word with him, I'll tell him what's happened."

He saw my juvenile consternation.

"I'm joking. Don't mind me. I wouldn't do that. What you do is private. These locations are bad enough for tittle-tattle without involving - begging your pardon - a couple of kids."

In the event Desmond Dickinson's lighting needed no adjustment. He had been an inventive lighting-cameraman, one of his most notable achievements being the rescue in 1943 of *Men of Two Worlds*, a drama set in Tanganyika intended to counter German propaganda against Britain's role as an imperialist power. Technicolor had refused to allow any of its four three-strip cameras out of the Great Britain during war-time and so Dickinson was forced to use the inferior monopak colour stock in the studio's own portable cameras. Already stale when sent to Africa, the film was virtually unusable by the time it had been processed in Hollywood. Despite this, back at Denham Dickinson had rescued the picture by creating the bulk of scenes using the imperfect negatives to construct glass shots for background, which were then combined with live action in the studio, thus bringing Africa to Denham. Nowadays computers and electronics make this easy and few people remain who can understand just how complicated it was. Now the veteran lighting-cameraman had been reunited in Tripoli with sound-recordist Dudley Messenger with whom he'd worked on Olivier's *Hamlet* a landmark in British filmmaking in 1948.

The working life of a film producer is seldom without problem. Bill MacQuitty was no exception. An elaborate tank battle scene was a vital part of the wide-screen vista. This is where the hero would die. The golden sands of the Gafara Plain at Aziza some miles from Tripoli and a barren part of the desert had been chosen. Explosives

were prepared and buried. At the appropriate time guns and flame erupted, explosions shook the ground and sand and dust and equipment were flung high into the air. It was all extremely satisfying and the producer could take pride that this vital high point would explode on Odeon screens across the land. Throughout the spectacle a tall distinguished robed figure stood beside him. As the dust settled he spoke quietly to the producer.
"Why Sire do you destroy my cornfields?"

The vastness that is the Sahara has been variously estimated at between seven and nine million square kilometres or one-third the size of Africa. Countless miles of sand from coast to coast. But apparently the producer had chosen just that bit which had been planted. MacQuitty protested vehemently. There could have been no greater preparation, every opportunity had been made for objections. This was just arid desert. The figure shook his head and continued with dignity. Allah knew better. With His Grace when the rains came in February the corn he had planted would spring up, but now the Effendi had blown it all away.

How many cups of coffee were drunk, how many courteous exchanges took place with this quiet dignified Bedouin is not known but the unit accounts eventually showed an incidental of £200 and the matter was settled with honour. It was not the only cultural misunderstanding between the generous Irishman and the desert-people. Art Director George Provis designed a beautiful pool for the pre-nuptial bathing scene, the location oasis having only a small well. MacQuitty was aware that the pool would ever after be a useful water supply for the Bedouin and instructed that it be made strongly for permanency. The village headman saw the producer's generosity differently, the concrete pool desecrated the oasis and must be removed. It was – and the Sahara regained a hundred square metres of lost sand.

We were scheduled to film a duologue between the boy and his uncle and it immediately became clear that from the actors' point of view two major obstacles were present. The first of these was the ever present sand blown on the wind, but with an expensive Vistavision camera to protect no one was much interested in the actors' crevices. The other problem was flies, buzzing noisily and landing on the actors' faces. Producer MacQuitty, no doubt with an eye on time and his budget, proposed spraying me with flyspray immediately before each take. "You'll kill the lad!" was the protest from BDH, uncharacteristically caring of his actor.

The desert wind known as *ghibli* had been increasing through the day, yet it brought no respite from the stifling heat. In the nearby port a ship moaned its foghorn call. The wind in the palms played shadow pictures on the wall above my bed bringing strange animation to the background of the noise of the chatter of countless locusts. At seven o'clock three hours before, from the top of the nearby minaret the muezin had made the final prayer call of the day. Now the nocturnal silence was broken only by the night noises of Africa and the rasping of sand against the window.

Rosemarie squealed.

"What's the matter, have I hurt you?" I eased my weight.

"No. You......you twitched." She looked up at me, with wide eyes.

"Oh that. I thought you'd like it."

"I didn't say I didn't like it, but why do you do it?"

"My grandmother told me to. She said never just roll over and go to sleep. And always give a twitch so the lady knows you're awake."

"Your grandmother told you that!"

"Not really. I read it somewhere. But people might think it a bit pervy reading books like that."

"Some people might think the pervy bit was discussing it with your grandmother!"

She lay silently for a moment in the darkness, contemplating the ceiling, where the moonlight shimmered its reflection from the pool below.

"Can I ask you something?" she murmered.

"Ask away. Whatever you like"

"It's just that I'm worried."

"What about?"

"Well you know when you kissed me, after the ball. All over, and you kissed my thighs and…"

Despite the heat I went cold. "Oh God, I felt you tense up, you didn't like it!"

She shook her head. "I liked it very much."

"Then I don't understand. What's the problem?"

"It's just that I don't do it for you."

"Well, is that a problem?"

"It just seems so…well selfish."

"It's not selfish at all. You know what you feel. And if something's not good for you….. well it's not good for me either."

"Is that what your grandmother said?"

"No it's what I said. And I mean it. Now do you feel better?"

"A bit."

"Then go to sleep and stop worrying about things that aren't important."

"You mean that Terry? Really, you don't mind?"

"Absolutely." I put my hand on my heart, "I mean it - *sincerely*."

A moment later she was asleep, her bosom rising and falling and catching the light from the window, the warmth from her steady breathing tracing patterns on my neck. I closed my eyes against her nakedness. As the great Olivier once said, "The key to acting is sincerity. Once you can fake that, you're set."

It was my turn to contemplate the ceiling.

Sir Laurence would have been proud of me tonight.

ಸಂಬ

Chapter six

Wheelus Field USAAF

From our twenty-first century perspective it is difficult to visualise a Tripoli as other than smouldering and burnt-out buildings, and armed gangs in the debris-strewn streets. But go back beyond 2011 and the civil war to oust Muammar Ghaddafi. Beyond the Colonel's 1969 coup. Beyond the discovery of oil in 1959 which transformed the country's fortunes. Beyond the United Nation's resolution of 1949 making Tripoli an independent kingdom and appointing a king. Go back beyond the British Eighth Army seizure of Libya from the Italians in January 1943 and a very different Tripoli is seen. These were the heady pre-war days of an elegant sophisticated city of gardens and fountains and tall white buildings and magnificent hotels. All this as part of Dictator Mussolini's grand plan, not only to reflect the might of fascist Italy just three hundred miles across the Mediterranean but also to attract tourists to its Libyan colony.

As part of this plan the Dictator determined to use the sport of motor-racing to enhance Italy's reputation on the world stage. Racing had been a regular sport since 1925 but a dozen or so drivers on a 26km slow and unchallenging circuit attracted little local support let alone international interest. Mussolini was determined to change all this. In 1933 on the centuries-old salt lake at Mellaha six miles east of the city he built a new circuit eight and a quarter miles long, the fastest in the world. Its start/finish line was dominated by a tall white control tower and a vast 10,000 seater grandstand with cantilevered roof of reinforced concrete, the first of its kind. There had been no racing since 1930 and it was clear to Mussolini's publicists that reviving interest in the sport would be challenging. It was not sufficient to say that there would be thirty world-class drivers on the starting grid, or that the new track with long straights and undulating curves would ensure repeated views of the 120 mph flat-out driving over thirty laps, whether seated in the stadium or watching from the dusty trackside. Something more was needed.

The publicists were not alone in this concern. Signor Giovanni Canestrini the editor of a leading Italian sporting newspaper found inspiration in the horse-racing world where the new government of the Irish Free State had begun a hospitals sweep-stake a couple of years before. The chance to become the holder of a lottery ticket with the name of a horse which might then win the major race had been seized upon by millions, not only in the auld country but in lands far beyond the Irish Sea. It had worked in Ireland why not in Tripolitania? Not horses but horse-power.

Canestrini's proposal was attractive and so the *Tripoli Lotterie dei Millioni* was born. Approved by Mussolini and King Vittorio Emanuele III (in the curious alliance of Dictator and Monarch that was pre-war Italy) the tickets went on sale in October 1932. AutoClub Tripoli was enthusiastic too since a million and a

Mallaha Race Circuit Tripoli
The fastest in the world in 1933

quarter lire was its share for expenses. Little did the organisers forsee that they were embarking on a route that would give the inauguration a history more chequered than the winner's flag.

By 29 April 1933, eight days before the inaugural race, one and a quarter million tickets had been sold and enormous interest had been created in the race. Some fifteen million lire ($790,000) is thought to have been raised by the 12 lire tickets. The thirty tickets bearing the numbers of the starting-drivers netted each of the winning ticket holders a $1000 prize and of course any of these winning tickets could make the final three. At six – two - and one million lire from the first three respectively there was a mighty 158,000 dollars for the star prize. This for the purchase of a 62 cents ticket. The thirty drivers on the starting grid translated to odds at this stage of just thirty to one.

**The magnificent 10,000 spectator grandstand
and state-of-the art control tower.**
Described by British ace Dick Seaman as the Ascot of motor racing circuits.

Enter Enrico Rivio a timber-merchant from Pisa who had leanings to reduce the odds. Indeed to remove them altogether. Rivio had drawn the ticket with the car number of racing-ace Achille Varzi. The merchant observed to Varzi the irony that if the Bugati-driver won the race, risking his life at 120mph (193kmh) he would actually take home less than the timber-merchant would with the lottery ticket. And so the plot was hatched. If Varzi won he could have half the lottery prize, it only remained for the driver to convince the half-dozen or so likely victors to join him in the conspiracy to ensure that he crossed the line first. Each would net much more than simply winning the race. (In 2015-income terms half of the ticket prize money was worth almost one and a half million dollars.)

Eight days later at the inaugural race meeting spectators were treated to a variety of unfortunate mishaps during the two hours twenty minute race. A car ran out of petrol a few hundred yards from the finish. Another clipped a roadside obstacle and retired. Other cars were seen to be limping along with spluttering engines. Varzi triumphed and took to the podium along with Tazio Nuvolari and the British Sir. Henry Birkin. But already race-officials were suspicious and next morning an extraordinary meeting was held by the Executive, charging that drivers Varsi, Nuvolari and Borzacchini had conspired. Others too were named as likely culprits. The President recommended disqualification and revocation of their competition licenses, banning them from racing. But these drivers were the finest in Europe, perhaps in the world and the sport needed them. They were simply warned. In subsequent years the lottery was drawn immediately prior to the race, making cheating much more difficult and the Tripoli Grand Prix would be among the leading dates of the sport until 1940 when world events ended its supremacy.

The circuit had encircled the Mellaha Air Base which had been built by the fledgling Italian Air Force in 1923. During World War II the airfield had been used by the Germans and then captured by the British. In January 1943 the United States 12th Airforce was in residence. It was an irony that the airfield built to protect Italians had now become the launch point for the 376 Heavy Bombardment group sending its B-24s to attack Italy. In 1945 it was renamed Wheelus Army Air Field in honour of a USAAF Lieutenant killed that year in Iran.

So it was that Rosemarie and I found ourselves at the guardhouse under the Wheelus Field banner a few days after the ball. Rosemarie had clearly been a hit with the hillbilly band whose members had invited us to lunch on the base. A military jeep had picked us up, its driver chewing and offering the obligatory gum, and we had been driven the fifteen minute trip to the air force base.

A few yards further on from the pistol packing, white-belted military police our passes were waiting for us and the jeep rattled its way over the tarmac beside twenty or more very business-like looking fighter jets with *US Air Force* emblazoned on each silver fuselage together with the country's white star.

"F86 Sabrejets" said the driver proudly. "See them swept-back wings? They'll take-on anything those Commie-bastards can throw at us – they'll out manoeuvre any of Jo Stalin's boys".

Stalin had died two years before and his successor Nikita Kruschev had appeared to adopt a more conciliatory attitude towards the West in an attempt to end the Cold War. Our Yank, if he knew of the demise of the despot, cared little for the changes and continued to extol the superior virtues of the Sabrejets over the Russian MiG-15s which he told us he had seen in dogfights in the Korean war a couple of years before.
"Ours do 800 miles an hour, you should hear 'em break the sound barrier".
"We did." Rosemarie squeezed my hand meaningfully.

I was fearful that the sight of aircraft so soon after the tragedy at Idris airport on the other side of the city would be upsetting but Rosemarie was enjoying the tour. The base was enormous, two square miles of HQ then extended over forty-two square miles of desert and was home to 6000 air force personnel and their families. The size was needed for its pilotless missiles range. The headquarters camp was surrounded on three sides by desert, making it a convenient spot for test firing their long-range missiles and the fourth side was the turquoise Mediterranean. The band was rehearsing in the base theatre beside the beach and it was explained to us that lunch was to be a cook-out which turned out to be barbecue-style eating under big sun-umbrellas.

At lunch we were joined by a couple of young teachers from the camp's elementary school and a large dog called Sergeant Bruno. He had a disconcerting habit of farting noisily throughout the meal until he was shooed away when to our astonishment he stood out in front of an approaching base shuttle bus, which stopped and he got on with scarcely a backward glance and took the seat behind the driver. It seemed that Sergeant Bruno was an unofficial mascot and was free to roam the camp at will, eating at the various cookhouses and stopping the bus when he didn't care to walk in the heat. We were told he always sat in the same seat and no one ever argued.

Sergeant Bruno and friend
USAAF Wheelus Field 1955

The camp had more than six hundred students and a number of schools spread around the camp including elementary and high. The two teachers had only newly arrived and ruminated on the hard iron beds and thin mattresses in their single room billets. Back in the U.S. promises had been made about Wheelus' standards of comfort which clearly the girls felt had not been kept, but they were cheerful and the subject soon forgotten. Food supplies were flown in from Germany but the teachers were not allowed commissary privileges. The Commissary was operated by the U.S. government under strict codes, and was a supermarket (although Rosemarie and I had never heard of supermarkets) selling food and cleaning-items at cost plus five percent. But only active-duty personnel, family or retirees could shop. The girls' had already found a way around this barrier and I saw a band-member hand over a large box of groceries in exchange for a wad of military payment certificates, that special currency used on the base.

One way and another the visit was a great eye-opener to us both, we saw goods on sale that hadn't been in British shops since before the war. In the midst of such plenty it was odd that our coffee came with powdered milk. Local milk was deemed dangerous and the army's frequent promises of pasteurised milk had never materialised.

The other thing that we found curious were the teachers' complaints about television. Back home they had access to several channels but on the base at Wheelus the American Forces Radio and Television Service transmitted Tripoli's sole television run from a small studio near the beach. The girls found it odd that there was no choice and that the station only transmitted in the evening. For our part we told them that it was no different in England where there was also only one channel, the BBC, whose black and white pictures were seen mostly on 12" screens in darkened sitting rooms, and it too was only in the evening.

Wheelus' Channel 8 programmes could be received in the city and I had watched them on the hotel's sole set, my first experience of seeing commercials which I found even more banal than those being made back in England. The Americans had had television advertising since 1941 but longevity was no barometer of quality. The most popular show was *I Love Lucy* and, in contrast to the commercials, its quality, both artistic and technical when compared to British tv situation-comedy was startling. Lucille Ball's production company used an innovative three-camera film system replicating the normal multi-television camera set-ups still used today but using 35mm film cameras with resultant picture quality far outweighing the customary grainy soot-and-whitewash output both from the early tv cameras and the infant telerecording direct from screens before videotape.

At the cook-out there was a lot of sport going on around us that afternoon including the permanent golf course provided by the MWR (Morale, Welfare and Recreation) committee though in golfing terms I suppose it was all bunker really since there was no grass. I am not a golfer but apparently a golf-club known as a sand-wedge was virtually the only equipment needed.

Five nights before, within minutes of the argonaut crash Wheelus had mobilised helicopters to ferry the injured from Idris Airport 26 miles away across the city. Two of the pilots heard we were on the base and came with an enormous bunch of roses produced at remarkably short notice. (It was whispered that a consignment for the wife of a high-ranker got her order from America a few days late that week). Tearful eyes all round including those of the two chopper-boys filled with laughter when Rosemarie discovered the bouquet was swarming with ants which had joined the consignment somewhere locally.

Almost everywhere we went there were reminders of the pre-war Grand Prix days in the asphalt racetrack surfaces, much of its eight-mile circuit had been incorporated in the roads and footways around the base. Over near the golf club by the eastern end of the base beyond its high wire fence lay miles of desert into which the missiles were fired and where an international incident was narrowly avoided when this naïve British visitor took a photograph of his beautiful companion. I had not noticed that the background included some tents and several large aircraft. This was tent-city with high broken-glass-topped walls, a place so secret that its personnel scarcely mixed with the base and were housed in large twelve-man tents. I still have the Zeiss camera which I had bought cheaply a couple of days before, just a museum piece now in our age of digital photography but I always remember that day when I had to hand over the film to the fierce military policeman.

Many years later the perils of wielding a camera in public places revisited me. In need of pick-up footage of an office building exterior I had been filming alone in a Buckinghamshire town. The police telephoned me at home having tracked my car number. What was I doing? Clearly not satisfied with my response the Law was on my doorstep within the hour. Over a cup of tea these Thames Valley constables muttered about "industrial espionage" causing me to become even more tight-lipped. A day later a woman telephoned to say that she was conducting a survey on police relations with the public and could she call? The following afternoon, this time over a glass of riocha it became clear that my filming of the building had attracted more than usual concern but she offered no explanation and we went our separate ways neither any the wiser.

At Wheelus, the military policeman turned out to be quite an affable sort who having executed his official task seemed more than happy to assist Rosemarie who had discovered more ants invading her blouse. Uncle Sam's Military Police are clearly up to anything the day throws at them and the Snowdrop produced some magic mosquito cream which he applied to her neck. His enthusiasm for the task knew no bounds and soon it was the turn of the visitor gently to point out what was off limits.

Apart from the loss of my pictures it was a memorable day with hospitable hosts, an air-conditioned day that offered a welcome contrast to the sweltering Sahara filming days that lay ahead.

ಐಲಿ

Chapter seven

London pride

The London railway terminus was a cathedral-like Victorian edifice that once would tastefully have represented the wealth of the Company to its shareholders and the safety of its operation to its passengers. Now it was just a worn out grimy building, its glass scarcely admitting the daylight and its mahogany woodwork unpolished. I waited impatiently for the train. At first I thought she had missed it. Steam had wreathed the arrival of the locomotive and then as it cleared she came running through the mist. There were specks of coal in her hair and I smelled the engine smoke as we embraced.

She drew her breath. "I look a mess, the window was open in that last tunnel and I couldn't close it."

I hailed a taxi. Rosemarie raised her eyebrows.

"Isn't this extravagant?"

"I'm celebrating. Last time I saw you was at the Grand Hotel Tripoli. I can hardly take you on the bus."

"Well next time we do just that, you're technically unemployed."

We had arranged to call on my old work-friends at the Saturday matinee. The taxi dropped us on the corner of Catherine Street, opposite the great pillared front of Drury Lane's Theatre Royal.

Rosemarie was shocked. "Look at the meter," she whispered.

It was true that the three miles had cost six shillings (30p) but like I said, it was a celebration.

**Theatre Royal, Drury Lane still little changed
from this 1896 view**

We walked in the shadows of the wide colonnades of the portico. The collonades in Russell Street have stood beside Drury Lane's Theatre Royal almost as long as the two hundred years old theatre itself. They support a covered way to the Princes Door, that special entrance created following a dispute in 1812 between King George III and his son the Prince Regent and still surmounted by the prince's coat of arms. The colonnade continues the vast length of the theatre's north wall from front of house to the rear. Arm in arm we walked together to where the columns ended by the stage door. Above the entrance a small window looked down on the street below, the window marked the dressing-room I had shared with actor John Harvey for almost two years. It's fair to say that there was much fatherly advice given and listened to and being with the older actor had taught me a lot.

The half-hour had been called, that curfew when all players had to be in and we had been joined by the room's other occupants. John's understudy Geoffrey Denton and Timothy Brooking who played the Crown Prince. John was almost a fixture at Drury Lane. He'd spent two years as the nineteenth-century sea-captain taking the English governess and her son to Siam and before that a similar spell playing an American naval officer in another Rogers and Hammerstein musical *South Pacific* which had arrived from Broadway in November 1951. The musical-writing duo had virtually taken over Drury Lane in mid-1947 when the theatre had ceased its war-time occupation as the headquarters of Entertainment National Service Association (ENSA) and the post-war gloom lifted with the arrival of *Oklahoma*. This had been followed by *Carousel* which notched up 566 performances before making way for *South Pacific*. Mary Martin who had originated the role of Nellie Forbush on Broadway came to London to reprise her part and the show ran for over 800 performances. The musicians' magic had brought a much needed brightness to a colourless London still drab and battered from the air-raids and more than a decade before the Smokeless-Zone legislation that would eventually chase away the yellow sulphurous smogs that frequently enveloped everything from October to March.

John ran an approving eye over Rosemarie. "Sit down my dear." The actor's dark-brown voice rolling off the distempered walls of the tiny room. "Goldie will make us tea." The idea of a woman dresser for we four actors had seemed strange at first but the motherly efficient lady had long become part of the dressing room team.

I left Rosemarie with the actors while I went to renew acquaintance with George one of the twenty or so stagehands who nursed the many scene changes and curtains each night. The Drury Lane stage is vast and is generally never fully used. What is seen by the audience is probably little more than a quarter of the area. I had scarcely been chatting for a moment when in the gloom across the back of the vast stage came Jimmy Smith. The Assistant Stage Manager was charming and well-liked by the actors but this afternoon there was no greeting as he strode purposefully towards me. "Terry, what are you doing here? Jack says you're to leave the stage immediately." Jack Waters, Stage Manager and God of this part of the theatre.

There is a long-established rule that visitors are not allowed anywhere near the stage in any theatre when the performance is on. I had broken the inviolable rule. No visitors. It was an understandable mistake. During the preceding two years this had been my workplace. It was so familiar that I felt I belonged. I apologised and returned to the dressing room, stinging at the rebuff. Decades later when I learned of Jack's death I had been ashamed that the first thing that had entered my mind was the memory of this censure of years before. But that of course is the nature of criticism, it is always first remembered. Jack was a kindly man and I had known him well and had learned much from him during my time in the show. It was entirely my fault but familiarity with the sound of the buzz of the assembling audience, more than two-thousand souls, filtering through the voluminous house-curtain, the scenery, the drapes, the very smell of the place was no longer enough. Outgrowing the part, I had left the cast – I no longer belonged.

I was indignant. Harvey was patting the spirit gum around his beard.
"Something wrong?"
"Jack chucked me off the stage. No visitors."
"Well I should think so too. You know the rules."
"I didn't think it applied to me."

The King and I. **Drury Lane 1955**
Photo: Angus McBean

Harvey scarcely looked up. When the curtain rose he would be lighting his pipe. Now he was placing carefully the three matches he always had ready poking out of the box in case the first misfired. I must have witnessed the nightly ritual almost a thousand times.
"Why not? Anyone not involved is a distraction. No exceptions."
I recalled the nights when the Defence Minister John Profumo had stood in the wings with fiancée Valerie Hobson, star of the show, throughout the overture just before the tabs rose on the ship scene.
"Jack Profumo did it all the time! He never got chucked out."
John was philosophical and surveying the tobacco continued packing the pipe.
"Sharkeybird, when you're a cabinet minister courting the leading lady they'll let you stand in the wings, till then you know the rule. It's not Jack Waters' fault."
The arrogance of youth wasn't convinced.
"Well maybe it should be limited only to people with an Equity card."
"That's nonsense. There are nine thousand members of the union. (41841 in 2016). That's four times the audience in this theatre. No Sharkeybird, you've got to accept it's a good rule."
"But OK to break if you're a cabinet minister?"
"That's right. Or if you're dead."
"What?"
"Dead. If you're a ghost. There's plenty on that stage downstairs. When you're a ghost you can stand in the wings." His eyes twinkled from beneath the peak of his captain's hat.

He was right of course - about the ghosts. I never saw one, but there were many documented sightings. The experience recounted by the young actress who played Princess Tuptim, a principal singing role, was very credible. Doreen Duke was an acutely superstitious and religious girl and had several good luck routines. Always she would wait as I exited over the side of the ship at the end of the opening and we would walk together behind the backdrop to the other side of the stage for her entrance a few minutes later. I got to know her well and the story she told me about her audition I believe absolutely.

With little more musical experience than the previous Christmas pantomime at Bradford she had stepped onto the vast, bare audition stage feeling far from confident. After her first shakey notes she felt hands upon her shoulders and a reassuring feeling as she was gently steered to another part of the stage. When she'd finished she felt a friendly pat on the back. Although she never named it she was convinced that she had been helped by some friendly presence.

Several years earlier Betty Jo Jones had joined the cast of *Oklahoma* in the comic role of Ado Annie. Initially, it was not a happy time for the American actress, her performance was not getting the laughs, try as she might the audiences remained unresponsive. One night she felt a gentle tug at her skirt and two hands upon her shoulders gently but firmly guiding her nearer to her audience and posing her body into a new angle. From this downstage position her comedy flowed and audience responded. Hence-forward she took the position indicated by the friendly presence and unfailingly got the applause.

Was it the shade of clown Joe Grimaldi who had spent many of his sixty years at Drury Lane and in 1828, too weak to stand had performed there in a farewell benefit performance? By all accounts this comic genius was a kind and generous actor and many think it could have been. Drury Lane is held by many to be one of the most haunted theatres in the world. There's been a theatre on the site since 1663. Currently the fourth, built in 1812 is said to have at least five ghosts. Whether it's Charles Macklin who killed fellow actor Thomas Hallam in a rage in 1735 or the more recent shades of Victorians Grimaldi and Dan Leno, reported sightings are frequent. It's not always sightings, sometimes the unexplained smell of lavender is thought to be that of Leno who always wore it.

Most actors are optimists so it is perhaps not surprising that such presence before a new play is always regarded as a good omen for a long run.

Doreen Duke, steered by some friendly presence
Photo: Vivienne London

Oklahoma, South Pacific, The King and I were all blessed with the appearance of perhaps the most famous of the Lane's ghosts, the Man in Grey. This tall elegant cloaked figure in powdered wig, ruffled shirt and tri-corn hat had been seen simultaneously by seventy cast members assembled on stage for a photo-call for Ivor Novello's *The Dancing Years* in March 1939. The glamorous giant chandelier for that production was still hanging high in the flys above us when I rehearsed there one April morning in 1955. Valerie Hobson was leaving the show upon her marriage to Jack Profumo. Her replacement Eve Lister and I were locked in a chaste mother-son embrace when the pianist stopped our duet in mid tune. "Bloody hell, look up there!" he hissed. As one we followed his gaze. In the third tier that was the upper circle, a grey figure moving with curious regularity could be seen. Jack Waters, stage manager was conducting the rehearsal. With trembling voice Jack called up loudly, "You, up there, who are you?" The wraith-like figure slowly descended the stairs between the rows of seats, leaned over the shining brass safety-rail and cried amiably, "I'm the painter guv. Was there something?"

Not every actor needed a ghost by which to be remembered. One at least from the previous theatre on the site left generous provision for actors coming after and ensured his place in Drury Lane memory. Robert Baddeley was a pastry cook who at twenty-seven became a highly successful actor working for the rest of his sixty-one years at the Theatre Royal. He left a £3 annuity to provide a cake and wine for performers of the current play each Twelfth Night; begun in 1794 it has continued almost without interruption to the present day. (Baddeley had not foreseen wartime rationing). I don't know how far that £3 goes today but the current owner Andrew Lloyd Webber supplied the drink in recent times. I was privileged to be present twice when this eccentric piece of British theatre folklore has taken place. No one has seen Baddeley's ghost but his spirit has a firm place in Drury Lane's history.

Baddeley Cake ceremony January 1955

Herbert Lom and understudy Ann Martin (covering during leading-lady Valerie Hobson's indisposition).   Extreme right: Myself and John Harvey.

My own audition one summer morning in 1953 had no spirit visitations. Indeed if there had been any spectres around I think they would have hung their heads at the hopeless cause of probably the most unprepared actor to try out on the hallowed boards trodden by such nineteenth century luminaries as David Garrick and Henry Irving and no lesser leading lights in the twentieth. A small fourteen year old boy I found myself on the vast stage squinting into the glare of lights fronting the lower circle. It was scarcely surprising that I was intimidated by a stage larger than entire theatres in which I had so far performed. From somewhere in the darkness of the stalls a voice addressed me. The contrasting blackness offered no identity to the voice. That it was American I deduced from my experiences of Tom Mix film matinées but this was no western drawl, this had more cultured timbre and with definite English overtones. John Van Druten, author and playwright had directed the first production on Broadway in 1951 and with the show's creators, Richard Rodgers and Oscar Hammerstein, was conducting auditions prior to repeating the task for the London production which would open in October.

I was relying on Shakespeare to get me through and had chosen John of Gaunt's famous – not to say hackneyed – speech from *Richard II* which I had prepared for a one-off performance, a month earlier at a parents show at school for the celebrations in that Coronation year.

"This royal throne of kings, this scepter'd isle..." in praise of England and considered by many to be one of the Bard's finest works reflecting his love of his native land. In the hands of a fourteen years old south-London boy it probably lacked something of the veneration accorded to England's greatest playwright. In the circumstances Van Druten, himself a world acclaimed dramatist, was patient and suffered the whole eleven lines to its stirring culmination *".....this earth, this realm, this ENGLAND!"*

Back at Clapham College the organ had struck up and the choir had exploded into Sir Herbert Parry's "...*And was Jerusalem bilded there in England's green and pleasant land.*" Which I, in my modesty, had considered a fitting finalé to my part in the school's Imperialistic jingoism. Drury Lane offered no such orgasmic conclusion. From the vast auditorium just silence. Stunned perhaps? If only at the remarkably inappropriate choice of audition piece for the part on offer. Again I squinted past the intensity of the battery of circle-front luminaires without success. From the blackness came the same mid-Atlantic voice.

"Thank you. Let's have your song."

Song? Song???

Now the situation was really getting outside my comfort zone. I'd never been asked for a song before. Beside me, at a battered upright, the pianist leant over.

"Where's your music, son?"

"I don't have any." All confidence gone.

From the stalls the voice, less patient now. "Let's hear you lad. What's the problem?"

The pianist came to my rescue. "A moment sir, just fixing it." And then, quietly to me "What can you sing?"

"Do you know *Home Sweet Home*?" I squeaked lamely.

"I think I can busk it" said the pianist, clearly up for a challenge.

I strode to the centre-stage mark and took a deep breath, at least I could try to *act* confident.

The pianist again. "What key son?"

Key? Key??? I didn't even know you had to bring a song to a musical audition, what did I know about keys?

He winked reassuringly. "I think *'G'* will be good"

Bewildered, I nodded. From somewhere the echos of the training by choir-master Brother Stephen and the centuries-old plain-chant of the school choir kicked in. Later I got to know the genial pianist well and he generously tutored my untried and unskilled singing voice. Somehow the song tottered to its conclusion and the pianist rolled out the final top *G* with an arpeggio flourish. I know it's a theatrical cliché but the voice from the darkness really did say, "Thank you. Next!"

Thus was my homage to Shakespeare dismissed.

When I left the theatre I could hear another hopeful, a twelve year old this time, stridently tearing the house down with a spirited rendition of *"I'm puttin' on my top-hat, Tyin' up my white tie, Brushin' off my tails"* while he tap-danced nimbly for the director. In the wings his mother smiled at me. It must have been his mother, only someone with maternal-ties could have smiled so warmly at the syrup.

Poor Rodgers and Hammerstein, it must have been a very long morning.

John Harvey had been instrumental in getting me my Equity card, without which it was impossible for an actor to work. At fifteen, the union had no procedures for admitting me to membership. John had argued long and persuasively with the Equity-deputy (shop-steward), one of the chorus singers. Equity would expect me to join at sixteen John had argued, so I deserved the union protection now, at fifteen. I don't know what the exact rules were but my Equity card was issued and for all I know I may have been the youngest member ever. Like many other British trade unions at the time Equity operated a closed-shop policy. It was not possible for someone to join unless they had sufficient paid work and most jobs were reserved for Equity-card holders. In order to allow new members to join there were a limited number of non-card holding jobs on regional productions. While working on these productions, actors held a provisional membership card and on completing the requisite number of weeks could apply for full membership and thereafter work in the West End or on film and television. Equity was the last of the closed-shop unions in the UK. The closed-shop was made illegal in 1988 and now a professional actor doesn't have to be a member at all and aspiring actors with sufficient paid professional work simply apply for a card.

**Eve Lister took over the lead in May 1955.
Our rehearsal duet was stopped in mid-tune**
Photo: Angus McBean

John had taught me a lot about theatre, the superstitions and its unwritten rules that could ensnare young actors. One of the greatest fears for any actor is being off. Missing the entrance to the detriment of the play, the shareholders, the other performers and by no means least, the audience. It had almost happened to him once and he'd never forgotten.

He had begun his career in Peterborough with one of Harry Hanson's Court Players companies. By autumn 1937 he was the popular juvenile lead at the highly respected Grand Theatre Wolverhampton in weekly repertory. This now long vanished form of theatre in which each night one or two performances of the play would carry on for a week, while during the mornings and afternoons the play for the following week would be learned and rehearsed. It was an incredibly hard task but it was a great training ground for any actor. Towards the end of his engagement there, John had sought permission of the manager, Basil Thomas, to attend John's sister's wedding. She had deliberately chosen Sunday the traditional rest-day for actors. The nuptials were to be in South London and John intended to return early Monday morning.

In the event the festivities were both late and great and, dreadfully hung-over, the twenty-seven year old didn't awaken until two o'clock Monday afternoon, one hundred and seventy miles from the theatre where the first house would start in four hours time. It looked hopeless. Even today with motorways it would be an impossible task. John was nothing if not resourceful. Croydon Aerodrome, London's airport in those pre-war days was a short taxi ride away, there an amateur flyer agreed to take him (for John's entire week's wages of seven pounds, ten shillings (£7.50)) in his tiger moth. Cruising speed of the bi-plane was under 70mph so time would be tight.

It was an open cockpit and John climbed up front of the pilot, to navigate generally by way of dipping down to look at the road signs to Wolverhampton where an unofficial landing was finally made in somebody's field from which John sped trying to stop any passing car. His popularity meant that he was soon recognised and given a lift to the theatre but even with this good fortune arrived only just in time. Most actors get one near-miss and learn from it.

It had almost happened to me too and I have wondered since if the audience, more than two thousand of them, noticed it. It was a December day and I was living with my parents in Great Missenden about ninety minutes train ride from the theatre. In those days domestic central heating was virtually unknown and grim smogs would descend on the capital, the product of millions of chimneys burning coal. In 1952 great public concern had been triggered when 4000 Londoners are thought to have died. A further 8000 died in the months that followed, leading to 'smokeless-zone' legislation a couple of years later.

But there were no such laws on that December day. The train was late getting into Baker Street and no taxi could have found its way in the yellow sulphurous murk. I thrust tuppence into the hand of a fellow-traveller and begged him to ring the theatre. Fog would not affect the underground. After what seemed like an age the familiar fruit smell came down the tunnel of the Piccadilly line and we had reached Covent Garden. I knew the area well and sped across the market's cobbled streets despite the lack of visibility. At the stage door Goldie was waiting and I dressed in the corridor to the stage. Gerald Smith my understudy stood by, pale and apparently pleased that I had arrived. Filtering from the stage I could hear the orchestra reaching a crescendo under Reginald Burston's baton. "At least I made it for the Overture" I said, relieved. Fred, Drury Lane's stage door keeper of many years was never flustered, but even he baulked at this. "Made it? That's the bleedin' second time they've played it!"

No time for make-up. No time for the red spot in the inner corner of each eye to make them sparkle. No time for the red shadow in the nostrils to make them flare. No time for the stripe of Leichner number 5 down the nose to give it shape. Did the audience notice these things or even that the overture had been repeated? I never knew. But it was the end of winter travel for me. Next day I rented a tiny flat, a scarcely converted stable in Notting Hill Gate almost opposite Hyde Park. Now if necessary I could run to work.

Through the dressing room Tannoy the stage-manager's call for overture and beginners was announced. Soon the first clear '*A*' from the oboe began the musicians' tuning routine raising the hairs at the back of my neck as it always did. John, now fully costumed in his role as Captain Orton, disappeared downstairs to climb aboard the S.S. Chow Phya which opened the show. John's understudy Geoffrey Denton poured more tea. The old actor's history had always fascinated me. His had been the task of singing in his wonderful baritone to the audience in the Windmill Theatre. The girls' nude poses could not move under pain of the Lord Chamberlain's rigid censorship rules. It had been Geoff's unenviable job to stand in a solitary spotlight, dressed as an old sea-dog and singing a sea-shanty while in the semi-darkness behind him the naked girls scampered off stage.

Needless to say the audience had not the least interest in this warbling Captain Birdseye as they clambered over the seat backs to fight each other for any newly vacant seat nearer the stage. I had always considered the job of comedian was the loneliest, especially when not going well. But I re-evaluated this after Geoff told me of his experiences.

Theatre Royal, Drury Lane 1954
Dressing Room number 10.

The third occupant was my opposite number in the play, Timothy Brooking. Tim had been steeped in theatre from a very early age. His maternal great-great grandfather was Charles Mayne Young a leading actor in the early nineteenth century who had himself played Hamlet at Drury Lane. Tim's parents were both actors, his mother Dorothea (as Daryl Wilde) studying at the Old Vic. Lately she had become a highly-respected television director of childrens' costume drama. Tim had spent his early years in Shanghai where his mother had a war-time attachment to the British Embassy. I have no doubt that some of those early Asian recollections coloured his role as the Crown Prince in the show. Many years later I was saddened to learn of my old friend's untimely death when at sixty-seven he was killed in a gas-cylinder explosion while restoring a lifeboat at Shoreham on England's south coast. Boats were Tim's passion and he had bought the craft to make his home, but with grievous injuries he never recovered consciousness and died six weeks later.

Finally Rosemarie and I took our leave and went down the Strand and into the Savoy. This had become my local pub before I was old enough to have a local. It was there in the vast Thames Lounge that the first- night parties were held for many of the forty-three theatres that then formed London's theatreland. The actors would sit into the wee small hours waiting for the first editions of the daily papers from nearby Fleet Street, eager for the reviews which could make or break a production. It wasn't the Grand Hotel Tripoli but I could see that Rosemarie was impressed. The faded gentility of its gilded mirrored interior didn't so much shout as whisper discreetly its fine pedigree. Dominating the centre of the room was the bandstand, a wrought iron gazebo like those in Victorian parks in the centre of which a dinner-jacketed pianist tinkled American jazz from a gleaming white grand piano. It was from a piano such as this that the American bandleader Carol Gibbons had broadcast with his Savoy Orpheans for the BBC's fledgling radio station 2LO in radio's early days thirty years before.

I caught the waiter's eye. Confidently I announced that we would like a couple of glasses of port. "Certainly, I will get Sir the list." His response puzzled me. Why did I need the wine list? He returned with what looked like a small telephone directory in which was page upon page of the Savoy's port collection. I have never forgotten this gracious man. He took one look at my ashen face devoid of its earlier confidence and ventured very quietly. "I think Sir will like the House port." I nodded gratefully. Such is the wisdom and understanding that keeps great hotels great. For many years afterwards I would always have the House port and it was always excellent.

I haven't seen the Savoy since its 2010 makeover when one hundred and eighteen years of panelling, gilded-mirrors, radio-bandstands and ghosts of fox-trotting dancers were swept away in a £220million refit, to be replaced by surroundings apparently more suited to our twenty-first century. I don't think I could bear to visit it, sometimes memories are best left undisturbed.

But I do miss the port.

ಸಿಲ

The four musketeers of dressing room 10
John Harvey (*Tunes of Glory* 1960) Geoffrey Denton (*Edgar Wallace Mysteries* 1960)
Timothy Brooking (*The King and I* 1954)   Myself (Posing 1955)

Chapter eight

The girl next door

Two years before this as I have said, I had fallen foul of the London smog and, no longer able to risk the uncertainty of the 30 mile train journey from my parents house into London, had set out to find a base near to the theatre. When first built in the 1860s the big houses that surrounded London parks were home to wealthy families whose several servants worked in the claustrophobic and crowded basements by day and crept to the attic by night. An upstairs-downstairs world of £1000 a year masters and £10 a year maids. Each residence had a garden at the bottom of which would be the coach-house, home to horse and carriage and with rooms above to house the coachman.

As the Great War to end all wars ended to be followed closely by the next, forcing historians to the convenient convention of merely giving numbers to the hostilities instead of names, so too came change to the coach-houses. The big houses had long since been sliced up into apartments and soon, with virtually the only remaining street-horses being United Dairies or Aerated Bread Company beasts, the largely disused coach-houses became the focus for landlords' change of use. Euphemistically described as desirable and charming, the leasing-out of the rodent-infested dwellings had begun between the wars and by the early 1950s were advertised frequently in the quality newspapers.

Elegant pied-de-terre. Easy reach West End.
Three delightful rooms.
Countryside in old Bayswater.
Luxurious mews flat with all amenities.

But it had been a card in a newsagent's window that had caught my eye.

> *More Rodine than Roedene. Shabby coach-house in colourful mews opposite park. Mile Marble Arch. Fully furnished needs paint. Usual references required. £20 monthly.*

Disillusioned by the time-wasting exaggerated claims in the newspaper small-ads that had been the precursor to half-a-dozen wild goose chases, here was one that had at least the ring of truth. Contrasting the brand names of a rat-poison and the elegant girls' school, the writer had even had second thoughts and had crossed-out 'desirable' for the more ambiguous 'colourful'.

A phone call and a bus ride later found me at the mews. The American handling it on behalf of tenants anxious to sub-let the unwanted remainder of the lease had been frank on the telephone. "They couldn't get on with it. They came from Dallas in the middle of the desert so what can you expect? They couldn't cope with the damp climate – inside the house. But for a British girl it shouldn't be too bad."

The trans-Atlantic assumption over standards of acceptability got us off to a shaky start, compounded by the American's surprise when we met.
"I thought you were a woman."
"Does it matter?" I challenged.
"Hell no." He fiddled with the key in the lock. "I'm just a bit surprised to find a schoolboy wanting an apartment."
"I'm not a schoolboy and my voice does this at the moment. Sometimes on the phone my mother thinks I'm my sister."
He pondered on this epicene for a moment. "How old are you?"
"Fifteen."

"Well I'm not going to ask why a fifteen year old wants to rent a flat but how are you going to pay for it?" His gaze fixed mine firmly.

Even more firmly mine fixed his. "Can I see it first?"

He evaluated the request for a moment and then ushered me over the worn threshold into the narrow passage that served as a hall. Damp-stained walls led to a flight of stairs which rose into the gloom.

"I guess no one ever thought of putting electric light on the stairs, you can get daylight through the door at the top but it's best to keep it closed because of the smell of the damp from the lobby. This is the kitchen."

I looked at the bare scrubbed boards and the empty room. "I thought the advert said 'furnished' ".

"Oh it's furnished alright, it's all in the garage."

Below us the garage took up the entire ground floor. Ancient stone, worn with the hooves of generations of horses, it had plainly been the home of motor-cars since the family brougham from the big house had been trotted away into the twilight of social history. Now the only witness to the room's former purpose was an iron hay basket high in the corner of the old stable, still with wisps of forage clinging to it, supper for town-horses long gone to final greener pastures.

I wrinkled my nose. "What's that smell?"

"It's cat pee I'm afraid. Most of the mews houses keep cats. You either get that or mouse pee. It's a bit self-defeating really. The more cats move in, the more the mice pee. A bit of Izal will soon cover it, though I prefer cats-pee myself."

Generations of children had skipped to the rhyme:
Ding dong bell, pussy's in the well,
Mummy's put some Izal down,
so never mind the smell.

And its fame as a germicidal panacea had been confirmed earlier when in March 1953 the soon to be infamous Reg Christie had used it a mile away in Notting Hill. He had pressed into service lavish quantities of the black liquid in an effort to quieten his Rillington Place neighbours' curiosity about the smell emanating from number ten. On that occasion however the product had not been up to the task presented by Reg's hoard of bodies in the walls, under floors and in the garden and the authorities soon got wind, literally, of the activities of the otherwise inoffensive necrophile.

The deal was done. The American's understandable concerns about a perceived schoolboy as a tenant melting at the sight of the advance rent. I followed him to the front door and stood amongst the collection of unopened mail on the mat. With a wave he turned the corner and I heard his footsteps on the ancient cobbles and a moment later the roar of the Cadillac as it sped away. As the sound faded I became aware of the silence of the mews. Only a few yards from the artery that was the Bayswater Road, a tarmac ribbon from Marble Arch to the dormitories of the western suburbs and beyond, yet in the daytime at least, the mews was a deserted and forgotten place. Though I was to spend the next two years here I never truly got used to this day-time silence.

One of the letters at my feet bore a Swiss postmark and was intended for the flat next door. It had clearly lain for some time among the catalogues and threatening brown-enveloped demands. The neighbouring property had been freshly painted and its bright yellow stable doors contrasted with the solid black cast-iron hinges and bell-pull. I could not guess at the age of the woman who answered my ring. She looked older than my sister who was eighteen. This neighbour looked about the age of many of the beautiful women with whom I worked so I decided that she must be about twenty-three. She was a neat blonde and her face devoid of make-up, glowed attractively. Her hair shone, not the brassy bottle sort, but deeply blonde down to the roots.

This was the year in which designer Norman Hartnell had raised the hems, broadened the shoulders and pinched the waists in pencil-slim outfits and my neighbour was clearly right for this time. A tight black skirt, with a tighter white angora top was only slightly covered by a red striped apron. Little puffs of white dust played around her flour-covered hands as she took the letter.
"This is for Fildelma my flatmate."
Her voice was soft, musical and Irish and her smile flashed like that of the girl in the Gordon Moore cosmetic toothpaste adverts.
"I'm your new neighbour." I declared.
"Ever so pleased to meet you I'm sure."
Strangely formal as she wiped the flour on her apron before extending an elegantly manicured hand.
"Is there somewhere I could get some sugar and tea and stuff? I've only just taken over and there's nothing in the house."
It seemed there was a general-purpose corner shop five minutes away and further away in Queensway, the mighty Whiteley's department store continued its eighty year tradition of serving the wealthier who, in these post-war years had tired of the meagre local provisions. Nine years after the war, grocery supplies were still sometimes erratic despite the fact that the food rationing imposed at the outbreak of hostilities had ended the previous year when the last of the rationed items, meat and bacon were finally lifted.

My guide, at her doorway, was interrupted by the smell of burning. Wisps of greyish smoke were rising from the window above us.
"Holy Mother of God. That's the griddle cakes."
She made off up the stairs beckoning me to follow. She threw open the oven door and thicker smoke, black this time, enveloped us in a choking cloud. She flung open the window wide and returned, pushing me out onto the tiny stair-landing. It was in darkness and

as she closed the door on us I was overwhelmed with the impression of tight space in the hall and even tighter space in my trousers. Standing in the tiny hall, her hands still on my shoulders I became aware of her delicate perfume. As my eyes became accustomed to the darkness, I could see flour on her nose and black smuts in her golden hair. In all of my fifteen years I had never seen anyone so beautiful.

After a few moments she gingerly pushed open the kitchen door and I was ushered into the small square room, a replica of my kitchen next door except that it was all brightly painted and polished with windows framed by lace-curtains and everywhere the unmistakable marks of an all-female household. The smoke was clearing and bright sunlight cut through the haze, glinting on her hair and filtering through the fluffy angora on her bosom with which I had now become quite transfixed.
"Do you know I've been cooking these for years, since my Granny showed me how and I've never done that before."
"I'm sorry" The perfume, the golden fleece of her hair not to mention the angora-covered breasts were taking their toll and reducing this youth to a mumbling wreck.
"It was my fault. Delivering the letter and asking directions."
"Not at all" the shining mane shook. "This place is too quiet. It'll be nice to have neighbours at last"
I tried to compose myself, steeling myself not to stare at her angora.
 "Well at least it's more troops in the battle of the mice."
"Mice?" the angelic face looked perplexed.
"Yes, the agent told me about the mice. He said disinfectant would get rid of the smell."
"Did he now. Mice? Is that what he told you?"
I nodded.
"Well they're bloody big mice dear. They're rats."
"He never said. Isn't the Council supposed to take care of it?"

She shook her head. "I went to the Town Hall but the problem is just too big. They said the bombs that had dropped in Mayfair had made the creatures move over here. Slumming it a bit - but quieter you know. Funny that, rats as evacuees."

During the war it had not been just the City that had been targeted. Although the City and East End had suffered enormous damage this had spread westwards into central London and beyond. During the Blitz more than 30,000 Londoners had been killed as a result of air-raids and thousands of commercial and residential properties destroyed.

A tea pot had been produced and soon the handful of tea was brewing in the porcelain. She motioned to a chair.
"Can't offer you a griddle I'm afraid."
My goddess was kneeling, peering into the blackened oven. "They're just burnt offerings, my Granny would be ashamed of me." She laughed merrily. Long red fingernails disappeared into thick oven gloves as she grasped the still-smoking baking tray. I gazed in astonishment. There on the steaming metal lay twelve griddle cakes, but this was no ordinary baking. These were as artistic as they were unusual. Smouldering in the sun lay the fruits of my beautiful neighbour's morning. Twelve Irish griddle cakes, each exquisitely moulded into the unmistakable – if charred – form of a life-size penis, erect and complete with scrotum. Granny had clearly been an unusually inventive tutor. Home cooking would never be quite the same again.

Although my beautiful neighbour never discussed her work, in the weeks that followed I eventually became close enough in my quasi-brother role to receive her confidences about what had made her leave her family and come to London, in those days a bold move for a young girl from a tiny Irish village. There was no doubt in Mary's mind that her journey from Ireland to London's West End had its beginnings at the little church she had gone to every Sunday of her life and in particular in the confessional there.

"Pray Father give me your blessing for I have sinned. It's four weeks since my last confession." Mary had closed the door of the confessional but was aware as she knelt on the rough wooden floor that the heavy oak had eased open behind her. She was familiar with its ancient warp and had closed it firmly but the wood found no purchase in the worm-eaten frame.

The shadowy face behind the wooden lattice was unmoved.

"What are your sins girl?"

Mary bit her lip. "Disobedience Father. She waited but there was no interrogation. "And I've told lies."

Still the shadow didn't move.

Nervously Mary pulled at the door with her foot. "And Father I've been thinking bad things."

The silhouette moved, casting light through the grill.

Mary blinked. The voice from the shadows was softly Irish.

"What sort of bad thoughts?"

"About boys Father."

"Were you now?"

"Yes Father."

"Tell me about these thoughts you were having."

The door was letting in the world again, a world of black-shawled village women queueing in the pews nearby. Mary lowered her voice "I think about them touching me Father."

"Touching you is it?"

"Yes Father."

"And where would these boys be touching you?"

"At school Father."

The shadow moved impatiently. "No, I mean *where*?"

"Oh here." She motioned across her top, as if crossing herself.

"Well now here's a thing. It's young Mary isn't it?" The lips moved closer to the grill.

The girl was surprised at this unusual breach of anonymity of the confessional.

"Yes Father".

"And you only twelve years old!"

"Thirteen last week Father."

"Well thirteen then. It's a pretty pass when girls of thirteen have such thoughts. What have you got to say for yourself?"

"I'm sorry Father. I'll do a penance."

"I'll have to think about that." The mouth was no longer in shadow and Mary recognised the fleshy lips and jowls of the parish priest. "Be off with you now child. Come to the presbytery at seven o'clock. I'll think about your penance."

Above the priest's desk in the presbytery the Blessed Virgin gazed from a dusty gilt frame. She had been highlighted in luminous paint and in the dimly-lit room cast an eerie glow which Mary had observed more frequently in Boris Karloff posters at the Roxy. The haunting eyes held hers until she became aware of a hand upon her shoulder. She turned to see the priest. "Good evening Father."

"Hullo child. Now tell me again about your sin."

"Well I have thoughts about boys Father."

"And you imagine they're touching your breasts?"

Mary lowered her eyes "Yes Father."

"Your breasts," the oily lips savoured the words. "Here and here." The strong palms pressed on the thin cotton of her blouse. The heavy gold ring was cold against her skin as the enquiring fingers probed the buttons. Mary raised her eyes. She could scarcely remember a time when she had not known her confessor, but she had never seen this expression before.

"And touching you here," the fingers traced the outline of the pubescent conical breast, pressing the nipple.

"Yes Father." A whisper covering her confusion.

The priest withdrew his hand. "And would there be anywhere else you might imagine yourself being touched child?" The voice half-hopeful.

"I don't know Father."

"Well, such as…. here." The wandering hand had reached her thigh, the scratching of the course serge of the school uniform unnoticed as the fingers crept towards their prize.

"Father, I don't think…" Panic overtaking confusion. The priest's breath was shorter now and Mary could see his neck, flushed above the stiff white collar.

"I'm thinking about your penance my child."

"Father, while you're doing that can you please take your hand from out of my drawers. I've got the curse."

The fingers stiffened and recoiled as the girl tore herself away, making for the door. The priest gathered his cassock around him and extended his hand, pontiff-like, after the fleeing figure.

"Ten Hail Mary's and go in peace."

"And you go and fuck yourself Father!" But the heavy door had closed and the priest, his cheeks glowing more brightly than the radio-active Madonna above him, was oblivious to the curse piled upon the Curse. From the oleograph the mother of all mothers looked down sadly at her errant son.

Mary didn't stop running until she got home. The only private place was the outside lavatory and automatically she began her ten Hail Marys but the third exhortation to "pray for us sinners" had barely left her lips when the rosary slipped from her trembling fingers into the metal can beneath her. The prayer froze on her lips as she watched the crucifix glint for a moment on the top of the flotsam and then, like a dying ship, disappear silently into the deep. There would be many more sins but Mary would never enter a confessional again.

There was a downside to not commuting. I didn't miss the daily train journey but I missed the people that I'd met. I had learned much from my travelling companions on the hour long journey each day. Six nights a week, homeward bound, I had run up the escalator from the Bakerloo Line underground and up the worn staircase to the street level platform of the Metropolitan Line. This was the oldest line on the underground anywhere in the world. From central London, trains entering Baker Street would emerge from the tunnel where almost a century before, the navvies had constructed the cut-and-cover railway track under the Euston Road. I would join the train to go westwards to the suburbs and the green Chiltern hills.

In those days the Metropolitian Line went forty miles out to Aylesbury, with wooden pre-war coaches each comprising separate compartments for eight, with slam doors and no corridor. Half-way at Rickmansworth the diesel electric locomotive would untie and a steam engine would take over for the remaining several stations of the twenty miles to Aylebury. By 21st century standards all very primitive but it worked and was punctual (except in the fogs).

I had not been travelling the route for long when an elderly gentleman would regularly share the carriage with me. Each night he would perform the same ritual, he would take off his weighty overcoat and homburg hat and place them together on the luggage rack above. Only the battered briefcase never left his grip. After a few nights he questioned me. He had been puzzled by the regular late night appearance of what appeared to be a twelve year old boy on the 11.00pm out of Baker Street. I recognised the old gentleman. This was Mr. Attlee. He had been Prime Minister for several years after the war until late in 1951 when Churchill wrested back the office from him. Now he was leader of Her Majesty's Opposition.

This was the lawyer, World War I soldier, injured in Mesopotamia, survivor of Gallipoli and the Western Front, latterly the Statesman who had introduced the vast post-war nationalisation schemes of such enterprises as railway and mines and the gas and electricity utilities. He'd founded the national health service, oversaw the independence of India, the end of Britain's role in Palestine and thwarted the Russian blockade of Berlin.

Did I ever once ask him about these things as the train rattled westward? Never. Always he would lean back, puff thoughtfully at his pipe and ask about my day and listen politely as I recounted MY personal events. Somebody fluffed a line.... An audience-member dropped a teacup in the matinée.... The trumpeter couldn't play for laughing. ... Oh the folly of youth. What tales I could have heard from this man of history.

The old warrior lived in neighbouring Prestwood. The village only had one taxi. Nightly the big pre-war Wolseley would pull out with as many as half-a dozen passengers crowded in the back. By general consent the elder-statesman would be dropped first then, again by consent, the youngest passenger – me.

It was a leisurely time that mid-twentieth century. Young boys felt safe, Prime Ministers felt safe. And if the occasional (and they were occasional) murder hit the headlines, the prospect of the Eight O'clock walk at Wandsworth and elsewhere discouraged all but the most foolhardy. The fact that elder-statesmen worked longer hours than fifteen year old actors was clear for although I frequently conversed with Mr Attlee on that penultimate nightly train from Baker Street, our paths never crossed on the way in.

If there was no matinée I would go into London around 4.30 and frequently a white haired old man in deerstalker hat would join the train about half-way through its journey. One Thursday he leaned forward and tapped my newspaper beside me. "Forgive me young man. May I read your copy of *The Stage*? Mine did not arrive today." His request punctuated by the rolling '*R*' of the old theatrical tradition, the mark of many a Victorian actor.
"And why may I ask are you reading the *Stage*?" the old man beamed.
"I'm an actor Sir".
"Are you a working actor or a resting actor? There are two kinds you know."
"I am working Sir, at the Theatre Royal."
"Haymarket?"
"No Sir, The Lane."
"Drury Lane. Splendid. A beautiful theatre."

It was hardly surprising that my travelling companion knew the theatre, he had himself played Drury Lane, for this distinguished jolly-faced man was A.E. Matthews, travelling from his home in Northwood to the Duchess theatre where the octogenarian was the star of the farce *The Manor at Northstead*. Mattie, as his adoring public knew him, had had an extraordinarily long career. At forty-seven in 1916, already a long-established theatre actor, he began a film career with the British Actors' Film Company. Unlike many, he had successfully bridged the transition when sound came a decade later. I am glad to say that because theatre was an interest in common, this train conversation was much more two-way than my conversations with the Mr. Atlee ever were.

I was privileged to have long conversations with the old actor, born in the 1860s he'd known Sir Henry Irving and acted with Ellen Terry. It was like touching theatrical history. The Duchess theatre was just down the road from Drury Lane and often I would visit him between the shows and sit enthralled at his tales of Victorian theatre. That facility amongst actors to bridge years regardless of age-difference when conversing, young discussing with old, is something that I've noticed very often. Mattie was a great character, his sense of humour captured for all time in re-runs on Youtube of his television *This is Your Life* in 1958, where he can be seen presenting host Eamonn Andrews a challenge to keeping the reins on time in those live tv days.

Under the headline MATTIE'S BBC FADE-OUT ANGERS VIEWERS the *Daily Express* reported telephone protests to the BBC. The Corporation apologised without reserve saying "it was clumsy and unforgivable. An unintentional mistake which we regret." The newspaper described the programme as "half an hour of the most human television of the series". Mattie, ignoring the fact that a tribute from Robert Morley in Vienna was on film, conversed with him about an up and coming new actor with whom the octogenarian was impressed. The newcomer was Rex Harrison.

Startled when Eamonn Andrews produced his birth certificate Mattie demanded, "Where did you get that? I'm off to Naples on Friday and they won't let me go without it." The certificate was dated November 22 1869. The newspaper went on to report how moved the actor had been by the programme, which it called *the* life of the whole series. It was clearly the night of his life and the old actor said so. "This is the greatest thrill of my few years on the stage. This is wonderful. Is there a good house out there?"
As Eamonn Andrews was closing the programme it was obvious that the actor wanted to say something. He got up and walked to the

footlights close to tears. He ran a finger round his collar. Then he was faded out.

In 1959, at ninety, the grand old man was campaigning to stop the local council putting an incongruous concrete lamppost outside his Georgian house. He made national headlines sitting and sleeping on the pavement to stop the desecration. It was said that on stage he would begin his first scene properly attired and then throughout the evening would gradually change so that by the end he was in his normal day clothes, devoid of make-up, poised to make a quick exit to catch his train. Drivers of fast through-trains would be persuaded to slow down at his tiny local station so that he could get off. A delightful man. If his appearance on the Piccadilly Line underground one day in his pyjama jacket which he'd forgotten to remove was mildly unsettling for me – put that down to my fifteen years – for Mattie there were more important things in life. He died in 1960 one of the few, true theatrical eccentrics.

Presenter Eamonn Andrews (1922-1987) looks relieved
as he steers the programme to its conclusion. 10 July 1958

If I sat enthralled with that octogenarian, there was another aged raconteur with equally fascinating tales of theatre's gaslit days. Drury Lane's publicity manager and historian was another larger than life character. Walter Macqueen Pope had spent all his adult life reporting on the plays and the theatrical gossip from London's West End from Victorian, through Edwardian times. By the middle of the twentieth century, 60 years old, he had a score of books on London's theatreland to his credit At almost seventy years old he embraced the fledgling television service and began his *Popie* series. Simply him sitting in an armchair recounting tales of theatre. It was radio really. But the television audience though small in those one-channel days loved the novelty of actually seeing the storyteller who held his audience spellbound with theatrical tales of long before.

Some years before I met him, the publicity manager had been walking with a companion in Russell Street beside the Theatre Royal in the summer of 1946 when ENSA was finally to give up its wartime occupation and the theatre was about to return to being a public theatre. ENSA's equipment was being sold off and a couple of purchasers were struggling to get a lighting switchboard into a small van. The companion immediately wagered "Five shillings says they don't make it Walter." The old historian accepted and the pair waited and observed as the purchasers struggled and eventually succeeded. Had they been less preoccupied with their task they might have noticed that the wager had been made by King George VI who honourably settled the bet with his companion.

Popie delighted in this story which he recounted while proudly showing me the Strand-Electric organ console which had replaced the ancient lighting controls a couple of years before. A Wurlitzer style Blackpool Tower type organ installed in front of the proscenium but hidden from view behind the prompt-side wall where, through a tiny window the lighting operator would 'play' its keys, producing – instead of music – fantastic lighting effects.

I had not been many weeks in the mews cottage I called my stable, when influenza took hold. There is probably little an actor fears more, especially when performing in a musical, than the dreaded influenza. In 1954 auditoriums were not festooned with loud-speakers and there were no face-microphones to amplify the actor's voice. The modern Sound Designer had not been heard of and actors would learn voice-projection instead.

Eight performances a week could be tough on vocal chords roughened from breathing the abrasive London smog. I stayed in throughout Sunday, the rest day, sucking Potters catarrh pastilles, inhaling friar's balsam and generally feeling sorry for myself. I had just finished repeating the rapid recitation "red leather, yellow leather" for the hundredth time as though its recital was some magic incantation that would chase away the evil (it didn't), when there was a knock at the door. Mary, my coleen neighbour, had brought whiskey and lemon and began to busy herself in the kitchen. She tut-tutted that clearly I had not eaten and came back with soup which she proceeded to heat. My neighbours were plainly angels and I felt blessed

A few months later in Soho's Greek Street I was startled to see Mary earnestly in conversation with a passer-by whose arm she took and made up a depressing shabby red-lit staircase. I supposed Fildelma was of the same profession. It was never mentioned and never once did I see them bring their clients home. They kept their work – at work. Mary had a taste for culinary skills and her griddlecake willies which she told me she kept for her gentlemen friends kept coming. It was the nearest we ever got to discussing work. I was fifteen and they regarded me as their little brother. The girls had hearts of gold and I missed them when Mary got engaged to a Duke and she and Fildelma moved away.

⁂

Chapter nine

Ghosts without greasepaint

Despite the ghost stories, in common with most actors at Drury Lane I never experienced anything spooky or paranormal during almost two years working there. But there occurred a not unconnected incident in the autumn of 1954 which has certainly resurfaced unexpectedly many times in my life in a series of happenings which I have never been able to explain.

The musical had been running a year or so and as I walked through the darkened fruit market beside the Opera House I was stopped by a man seeking directions to Drury Lane and the Theatre Royal. We walked along together, eventually I pointed out the front of the theatre and went on my way. A day or so later I received a letter from the stranger. Although I had not mentioned the play he had recognised me as his guide and wrote the following:

Jersey 22 October 1954
Dear Terence Sharkey,
By now of course you will have forgotten the meeting between a man and yourself who asked you to show him where the theatre was. I can only tell you how much I appreciated the whole production.

After some kind words about the play he went on:

Now Terence, apart from my work which is only bread and butter my hobby is healing people and as a clairvoyant I can tell that the power of Healing at present mentally is with you. From my seat in the Gods I saw quite plainly a North American Indian, a healer, but I think you will know more of this later in your life.

I'm afraid that my ignorance of the subject on which he wrote led me to send a simple reply and I thought no more about it for many years. Some years later I had been invited to attend the annual international Tiger Moth Rally at Woburn Abbey. For two glorious days the parklands of the Duke of Bedford's estate played host to the ancient bi-planes in an atmosphere that reflected the pre-war aviation age. The club enclosure was fronted by a large white marquee and from its lawn offered front row views of the world's biggest gathering of Tiger Moths arriving at the finishing line of a gruelling point-to-point across England.

The specially prepared grass landing strip had been part of a wartime runway for the Lancaster bombers flown there to hide among the ancient oaks. Although the grass extended into the lawn of the club enclosure, for safety it was staked out every five yards (4.6m) or so, with a rope dividing the landing area from the spectators. At each of the stakes a safety-marshal was stationed. After lunch the arrival of aircraft was spasmodic, every ten minutes or so. At one stage I saw a young woman, clearly puzzled, looking around at the crowd gathered on the enclosure lawn. She was elegantly dressed in Edwardian style and my immediate reaction was that she had adopted period dress to suit the occasion. Later, I recalled that the bi-planes were from the thirties, hardly synonymous with the clothes of 1910. When others said they had not seen her it made me question what I had perceived. Here was a woman, strangely dressed, clearly agitated, walking on the wrong side of the safety barrier and proceeding past the safety-marshals none of whom had stopped her or even appeared to notice.

Many years later I read of Lady Mary Tribe, wife of the 11th Duke who in the 1920s was a pioneer aviatrix. Known as the Flying Duchess she lost her life in 1937 while flying off East Anglia. She has been sighted in the grounds and always in summer dress.

....

With remarkable perception Winston Churchill ordered that an office block being constructed in Liverpool in the 1930s should include a top-secret operations room several floors underground. Closed at the end of the war it lay forgotten for forty years then the reinforced concrete bunker was rediscovered and reopened as *Western Approaches*, a museum of the Battle of the Atlantic in which it had been the Operations Centre. The visitor walks into a veritable time capsule. It was there one day in 1998 that I nodded to a figure dressed in dark trousers and a blue uniform shirt, he wore an official look and I took him to be a security man. He passed me and walked into a room with no exit. Only when I had left the building did I recall that he had not been in the room when I entered it after him. By now I had learned to question these odd occurences and three days later went back and spoke to the cashier. In answer to my question she said there was no security man employed and she remembered that I had been the only visitor at that time a few days before. In her words she and I had been the only people in that vast tomb-like cellar that afternoon.

....

From the admission queue at Howarth, famous home of the Bronte sisters, one November day I spied an old lady in Victorian lace cap and metal rimmed pince-nez staring from an upper window. Did they have costumed guides I asked the cashier. She nodded affirmatively, setting my mind at rest. But then as she issued the ticket, "But I'm sorry that's only in the summer." In the room was an old oak slant-top display case, and there securely locked, was a souvenir of the girls' housekeeper; a lace cap and a pair of wire-framed pince-nez.

....

A family pic-nic on the river-bank across the Thames from Lord Astor's seat at Cliveden was the location for another sighting. On the other side of the river, Spring Cottage had come to national prominence in 1963. Lord Astor had rented the cottage to Stephen Ward an osteopathic physician. It was here that Ward introduced showgirl Christine Keeler to war minister John Profumo. I saw a young couple dressed in Victorian boating clothes which I recounted an hour or so later to my dumbfounded family. They had not seen the striped-blazered boy with wicker basket, nor the girl with parasol. (Remarkably a companion at our lunch had also seen the couple – and vouched for my description.)

....

Then there was the evil smelling old man in the Liverpool theatre, unnoticed by everyone except me. Several years ago sitting in the centre stalls at Liverpool's Empire Theatre the disgusting and overpowering smell of stale urine from an old man some twenty seats away across the aisle in the side stalls forced me to find the manager and get reseated. Then I noticed that those theatregoers still seated around the old man didn't seem bothered. A Google search later revealed the information that the figure and odour was well documented over many years but – and here's the curiosity – the manifestation had always been confined to the Everyman Theatre in Hope Street ten minutes walk from the Empire. Spirits have been said over many years to lurk in Liverpool's theatres but my experience of a peripatetic ghost seems unique.

....

In the late 1980s I was contributing to an encyclopedia of the paranormal being edited by a writer well experienced in such doings. Lynn Picknett had been deputy-editor on the classic magazine *The Unexplained*. I was writing on voices from the grave and we had been lunching in a Hampstead café. Crossing the road I felt a sudden urge to enter an antiquarian bookshop. There among the dusty leather-bound volumes sat an old lady. I enquired of her if the place had ever been a chemist shop. She seemed surprised and confirmed that when her husband had bought the place in the 1920s he had turned it into the bookshop it had remained ever since. After we had left, Lynn asked what had prompted my detour into the shop and I explained that as we passed I suddenly had an instant vision of a small boy running down the road, medicine bottle in hand, to climb into a waiting Victorian hansom cab. And in my vision I was that small boy. I countered her incredulity with my own. "How" I asked her, "can you not believe? You – the editor of an encyclopædia of the paranormal!"

....

An old actor friend of mine who had been at Drury Lane with me had, as far as I know, never experienced any ghosts there. But years later shortly after his wife had died, he was approached by a woman claiming to have a message. It appeared that his late-wife was concerned about her wedding ring. The actor-friend had produced the sealed envelope given to him by the funeral director.

Inside was a ring in most respects similar to the one he had given her twenty years before but with one exception. There was no inscription on the inside. He questioned the undertaker, who declared indignantly that nothing other than the ring which he had personally taken from the finger of his dead client had been sealed and given to her husband.

It was only when shortly afterwards the actor recounted the events to his dead wife's twin-sister did an explanation come. Just before her death she had confided in her twin that the original wedding ring had been lost and that for years she had worn a replacement, but had never told her spouse. In her final days she was torn with remorse.

Do these tales have substance? Do they speak of voices after death? I have an open mind but it does make you wonder. Did that stranger sitting in the gallery at Drury Lane all those years before, see something on the stage and give an interpretation of his vision that connected those personal unexplained events later in my life?

ಸಲ

Chapter ten

And all that jazz

By the mid-nineteen fifties the singing style of crooners of the thirties and forties had run its course. The crooner's light clear voice with jazz and blues intonations was losing ground. Though the likes of Crosby, Sinatra and Nat King Cole would remain popular into what would be termed the rock and roll years, many others fell, soon to be eclipsed by the vibrato-style of Elvis Presley and his contemporaries putting their more modern swing on songs. But Elvis had only released *Heartbreak Hotel* a few months earlier and in England there was still a huge void in the music scene. The cultural leap between the old brigade and the rock and rollers was still to come. But it wasn't at all a landscape without music. Curiously, although the young didn't want the faded crooners of the older generation it was to an even older musical form that many turned. So it was that I introduced Rosemarie to jazz.

Soho's narrow streets and its music joints were just a walk away from Drury Lane. Opposite Geoff Denton's old workplace the *Windmill* theatre was *Mac's Rehearsal Rooms*. The Musicians' Union was just around the corner and when not making contacts there, many jazz musicians would congregate in the basement rooms during the day and practise to their heart's content where the neighbours, (the ground floor strip-club and the boxing gymnasium above) were bothered little by the noise. The musicians never minded a casual audience and so I would often drop by in the day.

I had warned Rosemarie that it was not very fancy. Ham Yard was used by the nearby street traders to store their barrows and all too-often rotting fruit. The basement was reached by a seedy staircase from the street and we passed a pugilist with broken nose from the first floor chatting to a stripper from the ground floor. Rosemarie's eyes widened. "Does everybody here look like they've stepped out of a newspaper cartoon?"
"This is nothing, you want to see it after midnight."
And see it she did.
Rosemarie was coming up from her boarding-school almost every weekend and my purchase of a motor-scooter, thanks to Bill MacQuitty's employment of the month before, was glory. A duffle coat, wind through the hair in those helmetless days and a pretty girl on the pillion. What more could one need?

Mac's rehearsal rooms and *Mac's Dancing Academy* dated back to the 1920s when Ham Yard was infamous as a jousting ground for London gangs, where cosh and razor would sort out who would sell protection to the scores of clubs in the seediness that was Soho. By 1955 whilst by no means salubrious, the cobbled square that was gangland's battle-field had adopted a quieter mood. *Mac's* premises had a good pedigree. After the war Ronnie Scott's *Club Eleven* had opened there in 1948 for a short time until he moved to larger venue at Carnaby St. The *Moffat Club* replaced it at *Mac's*, but 'modern' jazz was struggling to survive in the still popular dance music craze of the war years (Ronnie Scott's successful *Club Eleven* was an exception) and *Moffat's* closed very quickly. By the early fifties, clarinettist Cy Laurie had opened his eponymous *Jazz Club* which was to become a magnet for traditional jazz enthusiasts for the next decade.

By night *Mac's* rehearsal rooms took on a different image from the afternoon impromptu sessions. Rosemarie and I had parked the scooter beside the fruit-barrows abandoned for the night, and made our way down the dingy staircase. A couple of low wattage naked red light bulbs swinging in the draught from the double doors scarcely pierced the smoke and general gloom. Cy was a jazz man in the New Orleans style and though he never got the fame and adulation of his fellow Soho-club owners Humphrey Littleton and Ken Collyer, his club and his six piece band was the liveliest, most popular dance spot for young people. There were the upmarket clubs like the *Embassy*, *L'hirondelle*, *Murrays* and *Pigalle*, great for special occasions but expensive and lacked the sheer energy of the atmosphere at *Cy's*

Much of the clientele was made up of students from St Martin's Art School and the dress code was simple – there wasn't one. Anything went. Rosemarie's eyes widened as a half-naked youth in drainpipes and sandals jived soundlessly with a girl in twin set and pearls. There was little furniture in the vast dark room, just a few tatty armchairs and settees that had seen better days.

Rosemarie left me for a moment and made her way to the toilets saying "I'm desperate." A moment later she returned. "I just saw the toilets – I'm not that desperate." True *Cy's* paid little attention to guest services, here the music was the priority, only the music mattered. The wooden floors were bare, witness to their dance-studio heritage. Power failure or amplification breakdowns were a regular feature of the Bohemian scene and thirst was catered for not with alcohol but with tea from the makeshift bar serving what was loosely called snacks but often amounted to no more than crisps and soft-drinks beside the lavatories. Most nights of the week the club would close by eleven but tonight was rave night and Rosemarie and I danced together long after midnight, spurred both by the lure of the music and no necessity for late night transport since I had bought the scooter.

Cy Laurie's Club, Soho
The simplest of dress codes

I was admiring Rosemarie's ankles as I followed her up the basement stairs to the street. We had no sooner reached pavement level then Rosemarie leapt back out of the path of a thick-set man being pursued by a spivilly dressed younger man in the drainpipe-trousers and long velvet collared jackets adopted by the Teddy boys. The thick-set man had nowhere to go and as he turned the younger man leapt at him, knife in hand. The assailant hand raised and fell again and with a sharp cry the older man crumpled against a warehouse door in the dim gas-street-lamp that gave fitful illumination to the yard.

The big boxer had come up the stairs behind us. "What's happened?" he asked of Rosemarie.
"That thin man, the Ted - he stabbed the big one."
I interrupted.
"No he stumbled I think We didn't see anything. It's too dark."
We were in the closed end of the grimy cul-de-sac that was Ham's Yard. The beefy-faced big-bellied man was sitting against the wall holding his head, while blood trickled through spread-eagled fingers. His assailant had made off into the darkness of the tangle of narrow streets that made up Soho's square mile. Back through the dark, rubbish-strewn streets and across the bomb-sites to Shaftesbury Avenue's brighter lit strip, where theatre-land met more seamy entertainment.

I took Rosemarie's arm and hurried her past the Windmill and along Archer Street.
"Rosemarie, never do that."
"Do what?"
"Talk to people about what you see."
"But he was the man we saw at the door- the boxer, he was just curious."
"No Rosemarie. He's a gang member. I don't know which gang has control round here, but if he thought you witnessed something against one of his, things can get sticky."
We had reached a run-down cafe in Archer street. This was not one of the glitzy Italian coffee bars that were beginning to grow around Soho since frothy-coffee had arrived in England a couple of years before, *Harmony Inn* was one of many formica-tabled greasy-spoon caffs, whose bitter chicory essence came out of bottles of Bev or Camp, its only virtue was that at one in the morning it was

one of the few cafés still open. A successor to generations of scruffy coffee shops since the labyrinth of tiny streets that was Soho had been formed from the Duke of Monmouth's estates two hundred years before.

Over coffee Rosemarie listened wide-eyed while I recounted what Geoffrey Denton had told me about the square mile. Just before I had left for Tripoli Geoff had taken me to meet some of the girls he had worked with at the *Windmill*. It had been a bright late morning in August and life was normal in the shabby streets that made up Soho's village. Geoff's work at the revue-theatre had given him an intimacy with immediate post-war Soho and, like the residents, he regarded it as a village, a self-contained community. Paint-peeling sex-shops jostled side-by-side with amusement arcades, tattoo parlours, strip-clubs and basement cinemas, most operating outside the law. Overburdened book racks groaned under openly-displayed girly magazines and pictures, mainly unregulated by timorous council and police action. A quarter-century later the Indecent Displays Act would wrap in modest brown paper the titillating images of bare-breasted girls, but for now these beauties dominated the displays. The Street Offences Act 1959 was still four years away and we passed many young – and not so young women – who were clearly street-walkers as Geoff and I had progressed down Frith Street to where it joined Old Compton Street. At the corner the old actor paused and took my arm. "Last time I was here was bloody scary. Almost a murder in broad daylight!"

Two men about forty had been involved. Outside a fruit shop on the corner one had been accosted by the other.
"Albert, I want to talk to you."
Clearly a believer in the dictum, actions speak louder than words the dark, thick-set man lunged forward and plunged a knife into the other's stomach and face. A man of few – if choice - words he was

heard to shout, "You want to be a fucking tearaway, how do you like that?"

In the scuffle that ensued amongst the scattered cabbages and peas the injured man wrested the knife from his assailant and in turn plunged the knife deep into his arm and slashed viciously across his face.

The protagonists in this unruly scene which disturbed the late morning village quiet were Albert Dimes and Jack Comer, known respectively to their friends as Italian Albert and Jack Spot. Gang leader Jack Spot was described as a Turf Accountant when he appeared at the Old Bailey a few weeks later. The forty-two year old was charged with possessing an offensive weapon and with wounding the Commission Agent, two years his junior. In their respective job-titles lay the seeds of their discontent. As Turf Accountant, Spot took bets on credit, for periodic settlement with his clients. A Turf Commission Agent would place bets on behalf of owners or trainers and was sometimes paid a small commission. Most times though their reward was obtaining the inside information from the principal's instructions which the agent would then use to his own advantage to back horses or to sell information to other punters.

On this particular morning Spot, it appeared, wanted to draw a line (preferably red) in this commission agent's plans. Early in August, Dimes had written to Spot telling him to keep away from racecourses. "A final warning. Keep away, It's about time somebody else had your pitches."

At his trial, prompted by his expensive Counsel, Rose Heilebron Q.C.(Later to be the first woman judge at the Old Bailey), Spot explained how he would occupy betting pitches at racecourses. In order to get a good one he would book several (for an enormous £300 – almost a years wages for many), choose the best one and let-out the rest. Through his Counsel, Spot protested his innocence. According to Spot, all the injuries Italian Albert had received were self-inflicted with his own knife because, said Spot, "I was trying to defend myself, he was definitely trying to kill me."

At Charing Cross Hospital, Dimes had received twenty stitches to a six inch wound to the forehead, through to the bone, a stab wound to the abdomen and thigh and minor lacerations on the chin and left thumb. A most revealing quote which told a lot about gangland-Soho was Spot's response to police questioning. "It was between me and Albert Dimes and nothing to do with you. It's our business, leave us alone to settle it."

In the event prosecutions against both men came to nothing. They had each been charged with grievous bodily harm (GBH in the street-talk) and charged together with 'fighting and making an affray in Frith Street'. As we walked the scene together a few weeks after what became known as The Battle of Frith Street, Geoffrey Denton had concluded his tale of the bloody fight with the moral. "It's a different world down here Terry, what happens in the Village stays in the Village. Never chatter." He drew his hand across his throat.

The Old Bailey trial had taken place in September while I was in Tripoli and I had heard little about it. Various witnesses including an 88 year clergyman had testified as to the blamelessness of either Jack Spot or Italian Albert and the two had walked free. Within days MPs were calling for a full police enquiry into what became known as the Jack Spot case and jail sentences were eventually meted out to various witnesses who had conspired and lied. Reverend Basil Claude Hudson Andrews had been - he said "particularly revolted" by Albert Dimes treatment of Comer. Not wanting to get mixed up in it he had sped away to Oxford Street. Later, he claimed, he had read newspaper accounts, the matter had preyed on his mind and he had contacted the Defence solicitor.

Though of course Rosemarie and I had no way of knowing it that night, a few weeks later in November, the octogenarian would again be in the witness box. This time facing a seven and a half hour ordeal at the Old Bailey trial of Rita Comer (Spot's twenty-seven years old wife) and three men accused of conspiring to defeat the course of justice at Spot's September trial. Cross-examined, the clergyman said "I told the most terrible lies on that occasion. It is awful having your sins thrown at you after you have repented of them."

The old reverend who sixty years before had published a youthful memoir '*South Africa. A brief account of the Country*' had later held a clergy appointment in London's Kensal Green for forty years. How the elderly vicar had come to support the gangland boss was not revealed but one wonders if he ever reflected on his connection with the seamier side of Soho in later life – whatever 'later life' is at eighty eight.

As a churchman, the evidence of the shabby well-spoken clergyman at Spot's trial had been highly regarded. His back-tracking on that evidence a couple of weeks later might be regarded as something quite spiritual, but the reality of his conversion however was somewhat more earthly. It turned out that Reverend Andrews after an exciting youthful mission in the goldfields of the Transvaal had discovered other excitements and settled down in the north-west London suburb to a series of liaisons. In his own words to the *Daily Sketch,* (denying that he had come forward for material gain). "I have come to try and undo the lies I told at the trial…..Any financial difficulties due to my change of address and my harmless flutters in the sporting world are only temporary, due to my age and inexperience."

This ingenuous claim of recent misfortune completely omitted any reference to the Reverend's bankruptcy in 1924, his various dalliances with ladies, married and unmarried, (he lived with one for twenty years) and his frequent recent rendezvous with prostitutes in the Bayswater Road (though surely not for carnal purposes?) The Defendants were all found guilty. The three men got jail sentences of one and two years. Rita Comer (Mrs 'Spot') escaped with a £50 fine.

But tonight that was still a few weeks away. The retelling of Geoffrey Denton's experience of the violence in Frith Street coming so closely after personally witnessing the bloody incident outside *Cy Laurie's Club* in Ham Yard had unnerved Rosemarie who sat uneasily in the shabby café. She pulled her chair closer to mine beside the chipped Formica-topped table. The *Harmony Inn* café one of the very few that remained open all night, to service gangsters taking time off to sharpen razors, prostitutes on a coffee break or just wanderers and revellers who happened in. It was a dreadful place, bare fly-spotted light bulbs swayed in the breeze when the street door opened and the dismal distempered walls had seen little redecoration. Rosemarie pulled a face at the bitter chicory coffee, a definite hangover from the second world war and barely drinkable in the Hobson's Choice that was *Harmony Inn* after midnight. On the pretext of nibbling my ear she whispered, "Let's get out of here Terry, it scares me." Scare her it might but it could have been worse. For all the unsavoriness of the caff and its habitués, tonight at least it was only small-time baddies relaxing under the ever watchful eye of Dixie France, who it was said kept a a great store of weapons under his counter in case of trouble.

We returned to Ham Yard and the scooter and drove out of Soho's cramped streets and down Shaftesbury Avenue into the circle that was Piccadilly, its gaudy advertising signs contrasting with the theatre fronts of the Avenue, dark again until tomorrow night. We stopped and drank in the atmosphere of after-midnight Piccadilly. I turned round to Rosemarie.

"They say the Circus never sleeps. Always something going on. I remember my father holding me above his head one celebratory night. VE or VJ day I suppose. Eros was all boarded up then. All I remember was the great singing crowds, oh and that Bovril sign."

I pointed to where the thousands of ordinary light bulbs soared six stories in a never ceasing replica of a fountain. (Although the beef-drink would eventually be the first Piccadilly neon, in 1955 the animated advertising was still incandescent domestic bulbs.) I could see the flashing and movement reflected in her big eyes.

"I love the lights here," she said. "Oh and it's not Eros you know. The statue is Anteros, his twin brother, the god of requited love."

I pointed to the news cinema with Eros blazoned across its front.

"Well *they* seem to think it's Eros."

This was one of the twenty or so that had sprung up in London since the thirties. Showing continuously throughout the day a programme of cartoons, travelogues and news to amuse those with an hour and a shilling to spare.

Rosemarie beamed, "Well they're wrong, it should say *Anteros News Cinema*."

I kicked the scooter into life and we sped up Regent Street and Oxford Street, over Marble Arch and into the homeward stretch of Bayswater Road. This time of night was notorious for the street-walkers who found the neighbouring Hyde Park a convenient business place and behind me Rosemarie kept shouting in my ear "Is she one?" as if I knew personally all the working-girls in the neighbourhood.

We bounced over the worn cobbles and stopped before the stable doors. There had been a number of car-thefts recently and I had taken to opening the doors and bringing my scooter into the garage that was the ground floor. The house was never free of the heady smell of two stroke petrol/oil mixture and it probably didn't do much for fire safety but at least the steed was still there when I went down stairs each morning. Rosemarie kicked off her shoes and collapsed onto the sofa.

"I'm sorry."

"What for?"

"Speaking out of turn. To the boxer."

"You weren't to know. I didn't the first time I came to Soho."

"I imagined it full of lights and coffee bars and dancing. I never realised how…well cruel and ugly it all could be. That poor man, all that blood."

"His friends were patching him up. Remember, he'll be doing it to someone else before the week's out. We won't go back to *Cy's* Rosemarie."

"But you like it."

"There's lots of other clubs and there's always skiffle in the coffee bars if you fancy a sing-along."

It had been a long day but perhaps because of the events in Ham Yard sleep was not on the menu.

"How did you know all that stuff about Eros?"

Rosemarie propped herself up on the pillow.

"Sister Jerome told us in Latin. Strange really, walking about with that sort of knowledge."

She has a man's name is she…?

"Is she what?"

"Well, manly."

"No of course not."

"Well she's got a bloke's name."

"Lots of nuns have."

"You mean you're taught by a lot of lesbians?"

"No, it's not like that at all."

"Well it sounds weird to me."

"It's not at all weird. They simply take the name of the saint whose attribute they admire. Our art teacher is Sister Luke because he is the patron saint of artists. Some take women's names. Our music teacher is Sister Cicely, from Saint Cecilia, the patron saint of music."

I was not convinced. "And Sister – whatshername –Jerome? She admired Saint Jerome because?"

"Because he translated the bible into Latin. It's all to do with the saint, not the gender. We even had one nun who'd been married."

"Surely, you can't be a nun if you've been married?"

"Well that was the rumour. She'd been married and he'd been killed in the war before they, you know, did it. Mind you, she seemed to know a lot for someone who hadn't consummated. I remember her saying 'Girls if you pay attention to this bit of the lesson I promise I'll tell you some of life's secrets for when you're older.'"

"And did she?"

"Well, once she asked us what was the worst thing that could happen in a relationship with a boy. We all said getting pregnant. 'That', she said, 'was the second-worst'. We couldn't think. And then she said 'Not getting pregnant'. She meant being barren, infertile. I suppose that harked back to her husband being killed. Sad really. And she was called Sister Anthony. Like I said, it's to do with the saint, not the gender."

"Well I was taught by Xaverian monks and there wasn't a Gladys or Penelope among them. All Josephs and Stevens and Peters. Brother Peter took us for Latin, but I never understood it."

"I like Latin." She took my hand.

"Are you any good?"

"You tell me." Her lips brushed my ear.

"No I mean Latin."

"Well I've done four years, try me."

I thought for a moment. "Honi soit qui mal y pense."

"That's French!" she said scornfully.

"Oh yes. I saw it on a sauce bottle. What about my old school motto?"

"Which is?"

I pictured the badge on the blue blazer I had discarded a couple of years earlier. "Concordia res parvæ crescunt."

"Well that's easy. It means 'in harmony, small things grow.' "

I was impressed. "Oh you're good. I did three years and can't even conjugate 'terrae terrae terram.'"

"You don't conjugate a noun. You decline it. You only conjugate verbs."

"Oh God! I'm in bed with a Latin scholar."

"And that's new?" Her blue eyes gazed steadily into mine.

"Well I only knew that one. Brother Peter."

"And?" she arched an eyebrow.

"Well nothing like that went on at my school. I'm sure I would have known."

"I'm sure you would." she said knowingly.

"What's that supposed to mean?"

She thought for a moment. "You're blonde and…..well, pretty."

"Me. Pretty?"

"I mean appealing." Then as an afterthought. "In a masculine way of course."

"I hope that's meant to be nice. I understand though, I did get some odd letters sometimes, from men who'd come to see the show."

"That's what I mean. What did you do?"

"Well I answered politely and I ignored them if they wrote again."

"You see! Who's a pretty boy then?"

"Are we going to have a row?"

Her hand brushed my thigh and she nuzzled closer.

"Not at all. And speaking of your school motto. I'll look after the Concordia if you'll take care of the Crescunt." Her finger-nails dug into my leg.

"Well I won't decline that."

"You can't. It's a verb." She raised the sheet and looked beneath. "Anyway I don't think you're in a mood to decline anything. Concordia res parvae.... Crescunt."

She drew out the last syllable in a way that must have had my old school's founder spinning in his grave in Bruges. It is unlikely that the Franciscan monk would have envisaged a convent-girl's inflection and definitely not her interpretation of the motto he had so carefully constructed. We wriggled down under the cover. If this was her idea of seduction it was a bit erudite for me. I had always been bottom in Latin. But I suspected I was about to discover things which Brother Peter's teachings had never revealed.

ಸಿಜಿ

**Clearly a small costume-budget for this *Winslow Boy*.
I'm wearing my school blazer.**

'In harmony small things grow'

Chapter eleven

Margaret

On October 7 the BBC Home Service was reporting news of an air crash in the United States. In bad weather a United Airlines Douglas DC4 from Denver to Salt Lake City had crashed into a mountain in Wyoming killing all 63 passengers and three crew. I tried to shield Rosemarie from the news but she was aware. She looked up from the soup she was stirring on the stove.
"I know you know, about the American crash today. You don't have to keep making-up reasons not to put the radio on."
"I thought you wouldn't want to hear. It's another DC4 like yours, it would bring it all back"
"It's not like that. It's strange I suppose but I just feel so close to all those poor people, those sixty-six from Colorado, the fifteen from mine. Thinking of them just makes me want to make the most of life. I was so lucky." She continued to stir the soup. "The paper said the accident report on Tripoli will be published next week. It said some of people were buried in Tripoli."

Six of the victims had indeed remained in Tripoli including crew members William Gauldie and Margaret. The young woman who had gone to work that sunny morning three weeks before and now lay in the sand beneath a simple wooden cross two and a half thousand miles from her native Ireland would have been aware of the risks that she and others took in their working lives.

Margaret Denys-Burton c1952
Rome's Trevi Fountain
Photo: courtesy of David Bateson & Family

This was the golden age of air travel. Immediate post-war flying had been rough and unglamorous but by the autumn of 1955 Britain was leading the world in the emerging field of post-war passenger aviation. While other carriers still had the noisy aircraft of pre-war design, passenger-jet travel had been born three years earlier with the arrival of the DeHaviland Comet making BOAC the first commercial jet airline in the world. Travel times had been slashed, pressurised cabins had reduced noise and on long-haul flights to far away places with strange sounding names the aircrew epitomised glamour. None more so than its stewardesses.

Only one in a thousand of the wannabees who applied to BOAC were selected for the carrier's eight week training programme and in 1948 Margaret had been one. BOAC's airline beauty stakes competed fiercely with its trans-Atlantic rival PanAm whose stewardesses were all gorgeous and overwhelmingly blonde. The United States airline had even gone out of its way to recruit stewardesses from Scandinavia where the additional cachet was that the blondeness had its origins in Europe. But the British carrier had one ace above its American competitor; gorgeous girls *plus* that unmistakable 'class'. A real air of Britishness was brought by the daughters of QCs and Harley Street surgeons, of peers and politicians.

Margaret had never talked of her background. Her father, Sir Charles Peter Denys-Burton, fourth baronet, had inherited his title on the death of his father a prominent diplomat, the year after she had been born. The rambling mansion of Draycott Hall in Richmond, Yorkshire had been the family seat since the eighteenth century and from it her patriarchal ancestors had run the coal and lead mines on which their fortune grew. Her paternal grandmother's ancestors had loomed large in Irish politics, Members of Parliament for Dublin and County Carlow. The baronetcy of her grandmother's side, created in 1758, had become extinct in 1902 with the death of her uncle Sir Charles William Cuffe Burton.

After war-service in the ATS Margaret had joined BOAC as a traffic clerk, then re-mustered to stewardess in 1948. Later, she had clocked-up more than 1600 hours in her two years with the four-engine Douglas DC4 Argonaut fleet, one of the Corporation's older craft. The aircraft had seen distinguished if unremarkable service in the US military as cargo and troop-transport aircraft before the hundreds of surviving aeroplanes were sold off to the world's airlines as the war ended. BOAC had acquired a fleet of twenty-four, together with the Handley Page Hermes, the mainstay of their immediate post war operation. Argonauts had been used on long-haul since 1949 and had provided a reliable if noisy service. In 1952 the BOAC Argonaut '*Atlanta*' had brought the new Queen Elizabeth back from Kenya on the death of her father, King George. BOAC had retired the prop-aircraft fleet when it had introduced the Comet as the world's first jet passenger airliner in

May 1952. The Argonaut had been phased out through 1952 but had lately had to return when BOAC's Comets were grounded two years later.

Only two years earlier the airline had ceased its Imperial Airways flying boat service from the Solent to Johannesburg and the Comet was to be a giant leap forward, stealing a march on the American aircraft construction industry. Almost twice as fast as its contemporary propeller aircraft, it had rewarded the company with almost forty thousand passengers in its first year.
But then tragedy struck.
Barely a year into this jet-age all 43 on board had been killed when one crashed on take-off from Delhi. Eight months later, in January 1954, twenty minutes airborne from Rome a Comet broke up and crashed into the Mediterranean, killing all 35 on board.

For two months the fleet was grounded. After sixty precautionary modifications flights resumed in March 1954. Sixteen days later a Comet on charter to South African Airways went down near Naples. The Comet's certificate of airworthiness was withdrawn and the once redundant Argonauts were returned to service. A year later, in February 1955, blame was laid finally at the new science of pressurisation. Metal fatigue in the elegant window design of the Comet was the culprit. Thin fuselage metal would crack and cause sudden catastrophic depressurisation. Of the nine BOAC Comet mk 1 that had heralded the passenger jet-age, five had crashed, three fatally. The Comet never fully recovered from this chequered start, the safer skies having been won by the United States' Boeing. Indeed within a year BOAC would sign up fifteen of Boeing's 707s into its fleet. The Comet 4 would operate on a gradually diminishing scale until the mid-sixties but no longer held the esteem of old and would still to be linked with major accidents. In 1977 a DanAir Spanish holiday package-flight crashed on wooded slopes near Gerona killing all 112 on board. Dan Air had bought the aircraft from BOAC a year earlier. A combination of crew-error and air-traffic control misunderstandings had led to the crash and aircraft fault played no part in this and future incidents.

To Margaret and her colleagues these grim statistics were more than stark newspaper headlines, often the crews were known to each other and loss was keenly felt. But she and her colleagues had been war-toughened. Grieving was for off-duty times, negative thoughts didn't get passengers off the ground. At thirty-four, Margaret (Gypsy as she was known) was older than many of her colleagues and they would often look to her for advice. Earlier she had been unravelling the tangled skeins of a relationship that one new stewardess had unwisely started with a passenger and whom the younger stewardess now found to be married. The airline discouraged such things but liaisons such as these were inevitable in a life where schedules could mean four or five days of sun, swimming and relaxation and an equal number of nights partying.

If Gypsy avoided entanglements both with passengers and crew it was hardly surprising. There were those in her circle who still recalled her father's indiscretions which had come to national prominence in the year of her birth. Barely out of his teens the young heir to the baronetcy had become embroiled with an actress, Peggy Tennyson. A couple of years earlier the Gaiety Girl had caught the eye of an army major and in March 1916 had married him. The following month the major had been wounded in France, hospitalised for several months and returned to England. It was against this gallant background that a shocked public heard how Major Lennox Galloway alleged that the young Charles Peter Denys-Burton had had an affair with Mrs Galloway, the erstwhile Peggy Tennyson.

The petition was heard before Judge Horridge at the Divorce, Probate and Admiralty Division of the High Court of Justice in

February 1921 and in the curious language understood only by lawyers, the Respondent denied absolutely committing adultery and that anyway if she had it was the Major's own fault. In the midst of it Charles, only twenty years old at the material time, whilst denying adultery did not defend the case. He was, he told the Court, living on an allowance made by his father.

The Court and the newspaper-reading public heard the Major allege that in July 1919 the two had gone to Margate. There in the Westgate Hotel, Westgate on Sea the Respondent had been seen in Charles' bedroom and he in hers. After four days the weary Judge decided that the actress had indeed committed adultery both with Charles and another named co-respondent. His Lordship had, he said, taken account of the great changes both in manners and morality since the war but he could not accept as innocent an older woman staying at the same hotel as a 'derelict boy who drank and behaved like an idiot' (Charles had been thrown out of a London hotel and his clothes retained for being unable to pay his bill.) The Judge, in summary, recalled that she was always in and out of the boy's bedroom, she took him to London and wined and dined him at Murrays Club and then drove about the capital late at night looking for a lodging with him.

His Lordship continued, "Picture this extremely attractive woman with a boy, who had no clothes for the night, locked alone for the night in a self-contained flat. There is only one conclusion. A more disgustingly lewd existence than hers is difficult to imagine".

The sixty-three years old judge did not indicate how hard he had tried to imagine matters more lewd and disgusting but his condemnation seemed somehow accepting of young Charles' behaviour, indeed perhaps even a little envious. Granting the decree nisi the Court gave custody of the couple's child to the Major, leaving Charles and the other co-respondent to pick up a hefty bill.

Charles had married the previous May at Marylebone Register Office. What Elizabeth, his new wife of nine months before, thought of these proceedings is not recorded. However what is certain is that she was otherwise preoccupied. On 16 March three weeks after Horrocks' judgement she gave birth to Margaret. Twenty months later Charles' father died. The 'derelict boy' had now become Sir Charles Peter Denys 4th Baronet.

It had been a busy coming-of-age.

༺༻

Chapter twelve

Fallen idol

In 1954 British cinemagoers rated Anthony Steel and Jack Hawkins as their favourite actors. With another matinée idol, Dirk Bogarde, Steel was the highest paid British film actor. The two were paired in the war drama *The Sea Shall Not Have Them*. Steel played the duffle-coated, unflappable air-sea rescue officer hastening to the rescue of Bogarde's Flight Sergeant MacKay, downed in an RAF survival dinghy. The cinema-going public couldn't get enough of their star. The following year he made *Storm over the Nile* as a disgraced officer eventually redeemed and in the autumn began locations for his role as Captain David Holland in *The Black Tent*. A Rank Charm School graduate and veteran of almost thirty films he was just 35. Yet from this zenith it was to be only a few years before his career would descend into the abyss from which it never recovered.

In contrast, Donald Sinden his co-star in the desert would go on to achieve great theatrical stature, a knighthood and considerable wealth. Steel would die forgotten by all but a few friends, his agent and viewers of afternoon television. Yet here were two young men, Steel at 35 Sinden 32, whose careers at this time were not so dissimilar. That Newton's law of what goes up must come down applies no less to show-business than it does to apples should have been apparent to Steel if only from his pairing a couple of years before with two fading Hollywood greats. In 1952 *Another Man's Poison* saw him supporting an ageing Bette Davis who played a murderous landlady novelist. That the actress was cast in what the *New York Times* critiqued as a 'run-of-the-mill British melodrama with verbose script and uninspired direction' is an indication of the rating of the fading Hollywood star. The film played as a double-feature and Steel and Barbara Murray were described as 'adequate'.

Errol Flynn was his teammate in the *Master of Ballantrae*. (1953). Although the critics were kinder, this was the last of Flynn's thirty-five swashbucklers for Warner Brothers. Movie-going audiences no longer wanted the history-based escapism of Flynn's pictures, seeking more realistic modern drama. The release from his contract marked the end of Flynn's Hollywood career. That these fading luminaries were perceived by Steel as any portent of the shape of things to come seems not to have been.

In Tripoli Anthony Steel was never far from a group of admiring ladies, it went with the territory, but if the world for the matinée idol was a playing field of beautiful women, fate had just bowled a curving ball in the shape – and what a shape – of another screen idol. At a film première earlier that year he had met voluptuous Italian actress Anita Ekberg, eleven years his junior. The former Miss Universe-finalist at 24 had had a few walk-on film parts and her career was growing. Within a year they were married.

The *Pathé* newsreel shows a big congregation but the the *Times* on Wednesday 3 May 1956 had just four lines.

Marriage of Mr. Anthony Steel

Miss Anita Ekberg, the Swedish film actress, was married to Mr. Anthony Steel, the British film actor, this afternoon in the Palazzo Vecchio, the town Hall of Florence.

From his first big break as a p.o.w escapee six years earlier in *The Wooden Horse* his rise to stardom had been meteoric. He'd even entered the pop charts singing *Jambo*, the title song from *Where No Vultures Fly (Ivory Hunter* – USA) in which he starred with Dinah Sheriden. In 1952 it was the highest grossing British film and had been picked for the Royal Film Performance the previous year. By the mid 1950s his rise to fame had brought him to the point of comparison with such Hollywood heart-throbs as Rock Hudson and Gregory Peck. But if the lift-off had been spectacular, the crash to earth would be no less sensational. At the height of his popularity with fans at home he turned his back on the British film industry which had given him so much. True, in Hollywood his blonde goddess had an assured career but it was no more assured than his was in England. His departure, breaking his contract with Rank, made him one powerful enemy in that organisation.

Shortly after *The Black Tent* première in the spring of 1956 he had left with his bride for America. If the British studio had seen him as their answer to the Hollywood leading-men, Hollywood did not share the view. Little work came his way and, worse, he found himself referred to as Mr Ekberg. Now the ex-Parachute Regiment Captain, son of an Indian Army Major and every inch a gentleman on and off the screen, became an intemperate drunk lashing out at photographers who persued his wife and – it was said – lashing out at the actress herself. Nights in police cells followed, it was all so out of character. By 1959 the pair had divorced and Steel returned to England. But this was the beginning of the swinging sixties, audience tastes were changing. The stirring war-tales with clean-cut, well-spoken hero-type had been replaced with monochrome kitchen-sink drama where flat caps and flatter working-class dialects ruled.

By 1962 J. Arthur had become Lord Rank and had taken a back-seat, handing over the reins to his bull-headed accountant who, save for marrying actress Dinah Sheridan had little time for the whims of actors. John Davis had never forgiven Steel for leaving Pinewood and there is no doubt that this harmed the actor's attempts to revive his career. When, with his marriage ended he returned from Hollywood, Steel found few employment offers.

I met him again in 1963, he was still in the company of beautiful women. The stunning thirty year old actress April Olrich had been filming her night-club singer role in *Battle of the River Plate* at Pinewood while we were shooting interiors several years before. She had been a gifted dancer with Ballet Russe from the age of twelve and later soloist at Sadlers Wells. Currently she was receiving rave reviews for her role as Fatima at Drury Lane in *The Boys from Syracuse*. He still had the charm and bearing but something had gone. Some spark, something behind the iridescent blue eyes was no longer there. The bonhomie that I had seen at Pinewood in the handsome matinée-idol was muted. There was an attempt to kick start his career in Rome where square-jawed heroes still reigned but after several years his name was fronting fare such as *Hardcore* and *Lets Get Laid*. Some stage tours followed in the

1980s and guest appearances in television series. But these diminished and the 1990s found him in a small shabby hotel in London's Earls Court and then in to sheltered accommodation in a graffiti-littered council estate in Northwood, west of London. In 1992, hearing he was ill, I wrote to him but it had been too many years. I received no reply.

And there in cinematic terms the final iris-out might have concluded his story but for the fact that one day in the mid 1990s he answered a knock to find David Daly at his door. Daly had been his agent and friend for thirty years but had lost touch. He was holding monies for the actor and had worked tirelessly to trace him. Concerned for his frail elderly client, Daly set about finding him somewhere more comfortable to live. Steel was moved to Denville Hall, an imposing retirement home for actors in nearby Northwood. He died there in 2001 'A sad story of riches to rags' was the *Guardian's* obituary.

Ten years later in a sad replaying of ill-fate his ex-wife Anita Ekberg, now eighty, was reported to be penniless and seeking help from the Fellini Foundation in Italy where she had settled. In 1960 her uninhibited sexuality had entered cinema history with her plunge into Rome's ornate Baroque Trevi Fountain in Federico Fellini's *La Dolce Vita* and it seemed appropriate that her plea went to the great director's charitable foundation. What became of the much admired ring Steel had given her on their marriage, a fine emerald flanked by twelve diamonds and said to have cost him $24000, is not known. There had been a burglary and fire at the actress' home near Rome in which both furniture and jewellery were lost and which it was said had contributed to her present plight. She died in January 2015.

I remember Anthony Steel as a charming, urbane and witty man with a generosity to younger actors and a liking for their company and I am glad that at least for his twilight days he was in the company of others who knew him and shared his craft.

సెబ్

Chapter thirteen

Dream factory

I would say to any young actor who drives through the gates at Pinewood Studios without getting some sense of occasion and history that he should go back and do it again...and think.

The simple wooden sign with the two words 'Pinewood Studios' under the man and his gong which fronted the Tudor cottage reception for decades is not the type of magnificent entrance found in Tinsel-town's Burbank or Culver City, hallmarks of the great days of Hollywood. The board marks a turn in the road near a quiet Buckinghamshire village and except for the green wooden sign a speeding motorist passing-by could almost fail to notice. This is a dream factory which takes writers' imaginary pictures, magically turns them into reality in turn to feed the imaginations of thousands, (millions if the producer is lucky).

Heatherden Hall, a grade II listed building is where it all began. The Victorian mansion was built in 1840 and had been a grand private residence until the mid-thirties when it became a country club. Shortly afterwards J.Arthur Rank went into partnership with its building-tycoon owner and the house became the offices for Pinewood Studios. Five sound-stages were built in its 156 acre grounds, half the area of London's Hyde Park. Shooting started with Anna Neagle in *London Melody* in 1936. Thereafter its fortunes were mixed. The war years saw it requisitioned first as as food store then for the Royal Mint but soon it was again making award-winning films aimed at raising public-morale. But within three years of the war ending the studios were almost £400 million in debt (at 2017 values).

Enter new Managing Director John Davis ruthlessly cutting costs everywhere. Out went the grand big-budget spectaculars, replaced by Norman Wisdom and *Carry Ons*, populist fare which turned Pinewood's fortunes around. And of course the famous *007* years were still a decade ahead. Davis masterminded the studio's salvation and ultimately began steering it into other hands. He died in 1993 and within two years the studios were sold to filmmakers more committed to riskily fabricating dreams than running the bingo and Butlin holidays then considered more profitable areas by Rank.

Six decades of the man with the gong has left in indelible imprint on Britain's artistic history and the actor who is part of it today starts at those main gates. Well to be strictly accurate, the main gate until recent times. The quaint tudor cottage entrance is no longer in daily use, and the man and gong are gone. The current soulless uninspiring high-wired security entrance like some continental motorway toll-booth is further along the road and lends little for the young actor's imagination. So Young Actor, get out of the car, walk back 600 yards and sixty years to Pinewood's glory days.

The start of interior shooting for *The Black Tent* had been scheduled for a cold December day much in contrast to the Sahara location several weeks earlier. I had scootered from my parents' home in Great Missenden twenty miles away. I presented myself at the mock-tudor entrance and was saluted by the ageing door keeper, well he raised his steaming cuppa as he waved me in. It was just after six a.m. and still dark and as I reached the car park my numbed fingers hit the wrong gear and instead of cruising neatly into the reserved space, the scooter snorted, reared up on its back wheel and charged at the fencing, making a huge dent in the diamond linking before depositing me in a heap. Sheepishly I got to my feet and considered myself lucky that there were no witnesses to this pasodoble – or so I thought.

When J.Arthur and his building-partner built the first four of their 34 large stages they called them A,B,C and D; each was fed from the long South corridor which linked them to the dressing rooms and make-up rooms. Nowadays it is bright and colourful with white walls and floors stretching for ever, not a spider web in sight as it doubles for hospital corridor and such like. The *Carry Ons* were just one of the productions regularly to feature this handy location. Half a century ago the corridor was much more factory-like. I seem to recall cream and brown being the theme and harsh lighting throughout its length including the approach to each pair of the heavily sound-proofed double doors that at intervals led off into the various sound stages. I made my way past the other stages behind which the plasterers and set-builders had worked their transformations. Japanese-occupied Malaya for Virginia McKenna's's forceful portrayal of the frail English typist taking on the Japanese military in *A Town Like Alice*. (*Rape of Malaya* in U.S. cinemas). Sunny Spain for Dirk Bogarde as *The Spanish Gardner*. A wartime operations room for Kenneth More's limping Douglas Bader in *Reach for the Sky*.

Then I was transported back a few weeks to the desert location. There on the giant sound stage was the inside of the tent exterior which had made up the location. Great carbon-arc lamps would recreate the desert sun and all the audience would be aware of was an actor walking from exterior to interior, just moments apart in screen-time, but weeks and fifteen hundred miles (2400 kms.) distant in reality. Such is the magic of the film-maker.

I wasn't to be called until mid morning and was absorbing as young actors do everything that would teach me the craft that created such illusion. The tea trolley had arrived on set and everything stopped. While I was queueing an attractive young woman was calling my name. She was a secretary from the production offices sent to talk to me about my travel arrangements.

It appeared that my spectacular arrival a few hours earlier had not been without witnesses. Amy had come to tell me that the producer had arranged that henceforth I should have a chauffeur call for me and would I please avoid using the scooter for the duration of my part in the shooting. Just like that. No fuss, no admonition that my stupidity on a vehicle I clearly had not yet learned to control could have caused expensive delay to the production. Just a promise of action to prevent recurrence. I never knew whether it was Bill MacQuitty exercising his producer's eagle eye or some manager lower down the end-titles taking the decision to keep me (and I suspect more importantly their shooting-schedule) unbruised. That night I was chauffeured to my parents' home and the Lambretta unceremoniously brought back in a studio van.

Many years later I was reminded of the stresses of production budgets and schedules when I was unable to get an actor insured. I was producing a film-drama and the broker had telephoned me. The production could be insured against fire, delays, actors' mishaps and everything - with the exception of our leading man. The actor was in his eighties and not in the best of health and insurance companies are picky about that sort of detail. It was too late to recast, in any case he was a fine actor and absolutely right for the role. He was a personal friend of many years and I felt ashamed in entreating the Director to be sure to complete the old actor's scenes first "in case anything happened to him." It sounds mercenary and insensitive but production costs have a nasty habit of running wild and proper insurance is vital. I bet 20th *Fox's* Walter Wanger felt exactly the same way when Cleopatra, in the devine but costly form of Elizabeth Taylor, kept sending sick notes from her doctor.

Next day the chauffer not only came early but by arrangement let himself in and cooked breakfast for us both, he'd been driving big stars for years and apparently always made the offer, invariably gratefully accepted as I had done. I felt very grand arriving at the studio's cottage-like entrance in the limousine but it didn't warrant any better salute. The old doorkeeper had seen 'em all and he simply again raised his cuppa in greeting.

My driver was waiting for me at the end of the day and we were just about to drive away when there was a knock at the window. The voice was apologetic. "I understand you're going Amersham way, could I get a lift with you?" For me, in that instant the difference between Hollywood and Pinewood was epitomised. For the face at the window was Rank's joint-biggest star, Dirk Bogarde.

He remarked that his car had not arrived and that he had been told that we lived in neighbouring villages and would I mind awfully? His worried countenance reprised every *Doctor* picture and a good many tense war pictures beside. I was sorry that he was dropped home first, as the thought of casually mentioning to my sister that the matinée idol was in a car outside was attractive beyond belief. My sister, like thousands of her generation had displayed the idol's pin-up posters on her bedroom wall from puberty to beyond.

Since his death many have berated him for his lifetime-secrecy about his homosexuality, often in mean-spirited comments from those who because they themselves came out of the closet assumed puzzlement or disgust at those who for one reason or another wanted to keep their personal life private. To me, that was his choice and should be respected. He was already middle-aged by the time male-homosexuality was legalised. In 1955 there were 2500 arrests and the prohibition on sexual acts between males was ruthlessly policed until the statute was repealed (at least in England and Wales) by the Sexual Offences Act 1967.

When cast as a homosexual the extraordinary depth of his performance should have told us something and for some I'm sure it did. But in the end it was *his* business. Toward the end of his life, cruelly paralyzed by a stroke and his wonderful voice affected, he is said to have been a difficult irrascible patient, but on that sunny December day all I saw was a charming, urbane and amusing 'hitch-hiker', exactly as contemporaries described him. Above all I remember the big star's modesty. I've worked in the United States and greatly admire the Americans but I firmly believe that in Hollywood I'd probably have been turfed out of the car and it would have been requisitioned on behalf of the studio's (joint) biggest paid actor by someone in the Front Office. But this was England and Dirk Bogarde….and Pinewood.

The next day Rosemarie came to lunch at the studio. The oak-panelled banqueting room and chandeliers from Hetherden's more leisurly age now functioned as the elegant dining room and bar of the studios. Waiting to be seated I spotted a nun pointing at the menu with a large rosary. Recalling a visit to her convent-school I nudged Rosemarie, "Quite a home from home."

" It is a bit like school dinners," came her whispered agreement.

At this point the nun put down the rosary, glared at her companion and said loudly."If that Piccadilly line train was any more crowded I'd have been on the fucking roof."

Rosemarie looked at me and raised an eyebrow. " ....er... Not".

Later we had drinks (strictly non-alcoholic) beside the baronial fireplace where Australian actor Peter Finch is said to have extinguished the winter logs in a most novel way in reprisal at being refused a drink after hours.

**An inheritance goes up in smoke,
assisted by the prop department's lighter fuel.
Donald Sinden and myself trying hard not to get singed.**
The Black Tent

**André Morell, Anna Maria Sandri, Donald Sinden
pitch in to help the boy decide in**
The Black Tent

Photo: *Norman Gryspeerdt*
Courtesy: Allan Essler Smith Collection
More at www.briandesmondhurst.org

ಐಒ

Chapter fourteen

Picardie

It's hard to believe that England once had an airport busier than its competitor London's Heathrow, yet in the mid 1950s that was exactly the case. All the more remarkable for the fact that the airport was in a bog 73 miles from London, its single runway on a piece of shingle next to a nuclear power station. Silver City Airways had been formed by an ex-R.A.F. Transport Command veteran just after the end of World War II to ferry cars and their occupants across the English Channel. By 1954 it had outgrown its base on the old First World War airfield at Lympne where the waterlogged grass runway was an ever present threat to schedules. Twelve miles down the Kentish coast at Lydd, Silver City Airways built Ferryfield and such was its success, (with more than a quarter of a million passengers annually) that aircraft movements soon outstripped Heathrow. Its most popular route was the cross-channel hop to Le Touquet on the French coast.

This was Dickens' country. A moonscape of abandoned shingle beach and tufted greenery. The novelist had described it in *Great Expectations* as 'a bleak place, a dark flat wilderness intersected with dykes and mounds.' It was there that the boy Pip was confronted in the cemetery by convict Magwitch. A century and a half later not much had changed as I nursed the scooter, Rosemarie sitting behind, along the narrow winding tar strip that was the road from Ashford.

The airport, despite its busy traffic movements, comprised just two squat single-storey whitewashed buildings, the first was the Reception which doubled as a cafeteria and a pre-fab that was the customs-post. We were nodded through and almost immediately were confronted by the Bristol Superfreighter that was to start our weekend in France. The aeroplane was new to Silver City's fleet and had increased the company's carrying capacity from two cars per plane to three and their passengers. Motorcycles and scooters were squeezed in wherever there was a bit of space which had both the advantage of not having to book and a single trip price of just £1. (Alright that's about £22 in current money, but it still competed well with the sea-ferries).

We ascended the ramp into the bulbous nose of the aircraft and took our seats in the rear of the fuselage for the nineteen minute flight that would take us across the Channel to Le Touquet. For Rosemarie, who still flinched at any sudden aircraft noise, it was a mercy that any sense of take-off or landing was minimised by the fixed undercarriage and the flying altitude of a thousand feet, virtually hugging the waves all the way. This cross-channel 'air-bridge' had been the brain child of Air Commodore Taffy Powell and the public had welcomed it not only as a change to the ancient war-battered car-ferry boats but also offered the novelty of passenger-flight when the annual holiday was Blackpool not Benidorm, several years before package holidays made flying generally affordable.

Silver City Airways, Lydd Airport 1955
The new Bristol Freighter increased capacity by fifty percent
– to three cars!

Just twenty-five minutes after checking in at Lydd we were driving out of Le Touquet's even more primitive terminal. In the 1950s it was not surprising that scooters were popular all over Europe with fashion-conscious teenagers many of whom were women. Unlike motor-cycles, scooter-riders both driver and passenger had no need of special clothing and were isolated from the repellent noise and engine-smell that were the very same attributes admired by decades of motor cyclists. In London Rosemarie had been enthralled by an Audrey Hepburn picture in which the star rode scooter side-saddle through the streets of Rome. Whilst England was still seventeen years away from compulsory crash-helmets, side-saddle riding had never been permitted. I wasn't sure that the French didn't share this sensible safety rule but Rosemarie was confident and refused to straddle the machine. "It's the Continent, they're more likely to think like the Italians than us."

Certainly as we passed the airport gendarme he simply gave a wave, a typically French long look at Rosemarie and shouted "Tenez la Droite Monsieur!" as I drove on the wrong side of a bollard.

My passport still had the profession listed as 'schoolboy' but this presented no problem to the genial receptionist at the Hotel Westminster who simply collected our Fiche de Voyageurs for the local gendarmes and wished us 'Bon vacances, Monsieur-dame', that useful and curious amalgamation the French put on a male and female together. Le Touquet had been the playground of the rich, both French and English, between the wars and by 1955 had revived much of that earlier leisure and gambling scene. Away from the main boulevard which fronted the sea however there were still many reminders of the German occupation that had ended a decade before in hasty evacuation battles as the Allies pushed the defeated troops along the coast of the Pas de Calais towards Belgium. But all that was a generation away from the boy and the girl on the scooter.

Rosemarie gazed around the vast oak-panelled hotel reception, its walls adorned with pictures of celebrated guests. From gilded frames Marlene Dietrich, Noel Coward, Edward VIII and Mrs Simpson stared out from the past, marking the hotel's timeline from its birth in the roaring twenties.
The wire-cage lift trundled us up to our room and Rosemarie sank onto the bed.
"Terry this is very grand. We could have got a B&B somewhere."
"Well it's a celebration."
"Why?"
I sat down beside her. "Two things. First the commercials job means I'm not broke and second, we met two months ago today – well on Tuesday."

The sudden realisation that that also meant the anniversary of the air accident must have shown in my face.

"Rosemarie, I'm sorry I didn't mean to remind you of the crash."

She rose and went to the window and gazed at the sea for a moment, then turned smiling her reassurance.

"Terry there'll always be anniverseries of things, bad and good. And all this is lovely."

We found lunch in a nearby auberge and afterwards walked along the seafront. Le Touquet had been a place of elegance and style, playing host to the wealthy from London and Paris. Edward VIII and Mrs Simpson escaped there when they could and P.G Wodehouse and Noel Coward had each set down roots there, at least in the summer. We strolled by the graceful residences which lined the promenade. Set back from these we were surprised to find a huge wreck of a building. That it had once eclipsed the grandiose properties that surrounded it was obvious from its sheer size and splendour, still apparent though the ruin stood without roof and windows, surrounded by great tangles of undergrowth and the unfettered hand of nature.

This was the once world-renowned Hotel Picardy. Five-hundred rooms on nine floors and another fifty apartments each comprising several rooms with its own pool had been built only thirty years before to cater for the world's wealthiest. Set in its own fifteen acre park the hotel had rung to the exhuberances and excesses of the smart-set partying between the wars. The hotel had taken its name from the local region Picardie and between the wars had been the jewel in Le Touquet's challenge to Monte Carlo and it had succeeded. Airlines had advertised day trips just sixty minutes from London's Croydon with the promise of ten hours of gambling and the Picardy was the *only* place to stay if you were very rich indeed.

379 LE TOUQUET-PARIS-PLAGE - Vue aérienne du Royal Picardy
(L. Debrouwer et P. Drobecq, arch.)   Photo Peccau

Hotel Picardy 1930

The front steps were still intact and we went through the shattered doors into the atrium that had been the reception hall. Seven floors high, each floor circling the atrium with stone balustrade and where you could look up to where once there had been the roof. From the reception, wide corridors beckoned, each one flanked by stone pillars topped by grinning gorgoyle. A remarkable and eerie sight confronted us as we made our way into the main lounge, one of a hundred and twenty. The room was dominated by a great stone fireplace large enough to roast an ox. In front of this, scattered as if in some wild party lay remnants of furniture; overturned wicker-chairs, a velvet-covered settee, a broken card-table. Ornate chandeliers cast their shadows in the late afternoon sun filtering through shattered windows framed by ragged curtains. Little eddies of dust rose as we crossed the rubble strewn floors.

Hotel Picardy 1945

Shattered doors on rusting hinges made way into the kitchens where vast ranges open to the elements had rusted but still by their sheer number spoke of the grand scale of the catering that once had been. Zinc-sheeted preparation-tables stood where more than a hundred chefs would nightly prepare banquets for the world's wealthiest. Kitchen utensils hung from hooks, great cobweb covered pans suspended, desolately redundant. In a cupboard Rosemarie found a souvenir on its paper-strewn floor, a sheet of writing paper with Royale Picardy Hotel embossed in gold and surmounted by the hotel crest.

Off the kitchen, the ballroom spoke of happier times. Rosemarie stood on its central platform and mimed a trumpet. "This must have been the bandstand" she looked around at the high ceiling, and ornate chandeliers. "What a time they must have had here," She called. "What parties." The vast ballroom had a mocking echo. "*Parties parties*".
I agreed. "Great if you had the money."
"*Money money*", The ballroom taunted.

157

It was impossible not to be touched by the sense of depression and hopelessness in the building as dead leaves swirled around in the wind that came off the sea and blew through the ruin, all the more poignant when picturing the atmosphere of elegance, refinement and sheer exhuberance that must once have been. We made our way out of the main doorway and pondered on the coat of arms above. In the battered stone, but still plainly visible the stonemason's words 'Neo Pluribus Impar'.
Rosemarie beamed. "That should be your motto."
I raised an eyebrow quizzically. She knew the extent of my Latin.
She took my hand and kissed me lightly. "It means 'Not unequal to many'. Not that I'd know of course. But I'm sure it's true."

I had promised to take Rosemarie to the Casino that evening, her first taste of gambling and since it was mine too there was no chance that we would wager anything but it was more the thought of experiencing an elegant contrast to *Cy's Jazz* den in Soho. I didn't have a dinner jacket but considered that the white suit, now dry-cleaned of the sands of Tripoli, would serve. Certainly I allowed myself a sense of pride with Rosemarie on my arm dressed in a great bell shaped skirt and tight sweater. The Casino was just across the road from the Westminster, we entered with a sense of anticipation. A smartly suited man approached. "Monsieur-dames? Vous voulez quelques-choses?"
"Nous allons aux les tableaux Monsieur." I indicated the gambling salon.
My response prompted a quizzical "Quel âge êtes vous?"
I sensed a problem. "Dix-sept."
Moving to bar our way he motioned to an officially framed notice similar to those I had seen in café-bars. His voice was firm. "Monsieur. Je suis regret. La loi. Vous ne pouvez pas entrer."

It appeared that the law had firmly set its face against teenagers in the gambling saloons of France. I pleaded our disappointment but the Maître was adamant. I don't recall at what point Rosemarie took over from my schoolboy-French but the transformation was astonishing. Swiftly, we were ushered into a dimly lit room, a curtain was whisked aside and there through a two-way mirror we could see the splendid gambling hall. This was the casino that had been the inspiration for Ian Fleming's *Casino Royale,* his first James Bond, published two years earlier. A bottle of champagne was produced and two glasses with the longest slimmest stems I had ever seen, a far cry from the chipped tumblers at *Cy's Jazz* place. It was clear that there was no hurry for us to depart and we sipped our champagne as we watched the world of coloured chips, green baize and spinning wheel-of-fortune playing-out soundlessly before us. It was a tutorial for which I have always been grateful, never forgotten, but still I wouldn't know how to place a bet. As we left, our genial host pressed the half-consumed bottle on us, shaking our hands and crying loudly, "Vive l'Angleterre. Vive la liberation!"

"What did you say to him?" I asked as the December wind hurried us back to the hotel.
"I told him how my father had landed at Juno beach and had come through here with the Canadians and that this was my first visit to Normandy and I wanted to tell my Dad that I'd visited the nice places in town as well as the awful ruin of the Picardy. He said the British had been good to his parents and had spared their house. But I hadn't expected that hospitality."

I remembered how a few years earlier in Dunkirk on my first visit to France where I had seen tanks rotting in the sand, an old lady touching my blonde hair and asking, not unpleasantly, "Tu a etes allemande?" and seeing her smile relax and broaden at my reply "Non Madame, je suis anglais." My sense of the old lady's relief that I was not German, albeit of tender age, had stayed with me. In those immediate post war years the French always seemed pleased to see us, in contrast to the understandably cooler reception that the Germans received for a long time after.

Dodging the Westminster's dinner prices we found a café where an old woman was playing an accordion while her octogenarian husband accompanied her on violin. It was the first time that I had heard jazz played without a single brass instrument and the evening had sped by in a wave of choruses of *La Vie en Rose* and *Non, Je ne regret rien* lubricated by great quantities of rough red wine. The song had only just been written and though Edith Piaf undeniably made it hers in 1960, whenever I hear it I am taken back to a chintz-covered table-clothed café and an old couple who made my skin tingle at the very Gallicness of the music. No wonder its lyrics have never survived a translation.

Le Touquet retired much later than two tired English trippers but the town's night sounds did little to disturb the sleep that overtook us almost as soon as we got back to the Westminster. Later, in a half-daze I was aware that something had awakened me. Outside everything slumbered, not so my delicious companion for under the enormous quilt something was definitely stirring. I sensed a rustling in the linen and a moment later her head appeared beside me.
Her big eyes looked apologetic. "I'm sorry. I woke you up."
"I'm not. I'd hate to have missed it. But I thought that just wasn't your bag."
She settled her head deeper into the strange long French orellier that we shared.
"I remembered Bernadette's example."
I was perplexed. "I don't get it. Bernadette was the patron saint of the sick wasn't she? Lourdes and all that."
"I didn't say *Saint* Bernadette. I was talking about Sister Bernadette at school"
I was incredulous."She didn't teach *that*?"

"No of course not. She's our house-mother. I remembered what she'd said."

She disappeared below the quilt again and I felt her hair brush against my thigh.

"And what was that?"

The reply was muffled."Ab alio expectes alteri quod feceris"

"OK Clever! I'll buy. What does it mean?"

The explanation followed, even more muffled. "Do unto others as you'd have them do unto you."

I lay back on the unaccustomed foreign pillow as the night slipped away, but not so consumed in the moment that I didn't offer my own silent benediction to Sister Bernadette and her blessed namesake.

෩෨

Chapter fifteen

Adieu

The film completed on schedule and only the editing remained before its release in April. Cast and crew went their separate ways. I dreaded these occasions, the same whether in film or theatre. Goodbyes, embraces, promises to keep in touch. Many a tear and not only because unemployment loomed. This time Lady Luck was smiling in the form of my agent, Mary de Leon who had phoned shortly before with some commercials work.

Advertising breaks in TV programmes were just six weeks old and it wasn't only the viewers who had to get used to this medium. So too did the actors. There was a mutual learning curve. The commercials in those first months were very different from today. Centuries of newspaper advertising and scarcely a decade of radio commercials had not prepared the industry and its copy-writers very well. Generally aimed at middle-class audience, the adverts were longer than today and appear awkward and unnatural by current standards. In what has been described as merely newspaper adverts that moved, invariably there was a main and painfully obvious message as to why the viewer should use the product. Into this strange world in 1955 were pitched actors unaccustomed to the format and the performances were often not very subtle. This naïveté would not improve until someone invented the remote control and someone else invented colour.

The commercials had finished interior photography in a tiny studio in London's Victoria and were to complete shooting in a country railway station location. My task would be to extol the virtues of a particular toffee and its ability to sustain the weary traveller on long journeys. The producer in anticipation of the dawn-start necessitated by the script had us booked into an old timbered inn which seemed to have changed little in amenities or décor since the faded engravings of its coaching days a century before. During dinner I was called to the sole telephone. A tearful Rosemarie could scarcely speak. Her father's contract in Nigeria was coming to an end, he was about to start a new job in Texas. The company-funded boarding-school fees would stop when he left Africa and Rosemarie would continue her schooling in the United States. Rosemarie was calling from the telephone box outside the school, the three-minute pips sounded and the trunk-operator came on the line to request more money. I just had time to say that we would sort it out next day when she came up for the weekend.

Next day I had a half-day studio-call and got back to the mews after lunch. Rosemarie had made her way there earlier and let herself in and was waiting. She looked adorable. The fifties fashion of hoop skirts might have been created for her long legs, rising from slim high heels to disappear in acres of full nylon petticoat under the vivid crimson skirt.

She ran towards me. "Terry, this is awful. I should be happy. America! But all I can think of is us."
I too had thought of little else but was confident. "Rosemarie, I think I have the answer."
Her worried expression broke into a smile.
"Tell me."
"Look you'll be taking A levels this coming year. Can't you stay on at boarding-school over here for those few months? It makes sense."
She looked puzzled "I'm not taking *A's.*"

"Well *O*'s then."

"Terry I'm not taking *A*'s or *O*'s, not for two years."

It was my turn to look puzzled.

She reached for my hand. "I'm in the fourth form."

Things were no clearer to me. "Fourth? I thought you were in the sixth."

"Terry. I'm fifteen."

We stood looking at each other, soundlessly tears streamed down her face. In an instant the long-limbed young woman in clinging white angora sweater I had seen a moment before, seemed to dissolve into a young girl. It was only for an instant but one that would sharply etch itself in my memory. I cradled her tear-stained face in my hands and looked into her eyes.

"You never said."

"Terry, do you think it would it have made any difference?"

I shook my head, it needed no thought.

"No Rosemarie, no difference at all, but I wish I'd known that's all – I'd have wanted you to be certain."

"I was never so certain of anything. Those flames came so close. The fire finished it all for those others, I was so certain that I would never again place myself where I might die before I'd experienced what we have."

We went into the bedroom. She had unpacked her weekend case and her nightdress lay folded on the bed. She sat down beside it, idly playing with the filmy straps.

"What are we going to do?" she implored.

I looked at her helplessly.

"Rosemarie, I don't know. I'm shell-shocked. The fifteen-thing will fix itself next birthday, but this plan about moving to the States is different. And I thought I had it sorted out, simply just stay on for exams and college and university or whatever."

Rosemarie rose and knelt down beside me.

"I thought maybe I could tell my parents about us and you might let me stay here."

There was nothing I would have liked better, but the prospect of enthusiastic blessings by the father of a fifteen years old daughter who planned to move in with a shortly-to-be unemployed actor of seventeen seemed pretty remote. Rosemarie agreed and began to cry again. Above all I wanted her to stop crying, not only because she was distressed but her tears and vulnerability made her look less than the confident assertive seventeen years old that I had taken her for and pointed more to the reality of her years.

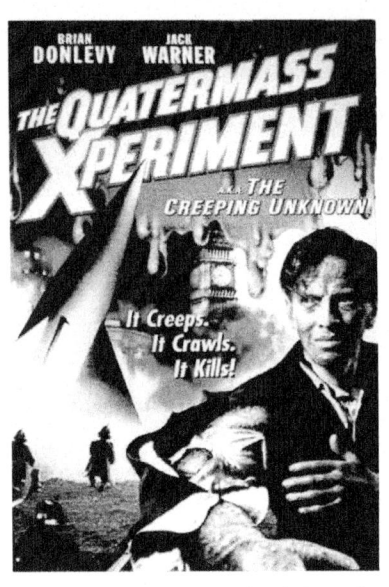

I wanted to take her mind – and mine – off the matter of age and suggested we go to the cinema. The nationally acclaimed *Quatermass Xperiment* (*The Creeping Unknown* US) had been premièred in August and was now making the rounds. Hammer's publicity department had dropped the 'E' from 'Experiment' and emphasised the Censor's adults-only 'X' certificate with spelling that featured a vivid crimson capital letter. As I bought the tickets beneath the poster with the great red 'X' I had the irrational thought that it was unlawful to take a fifteen-years-old into a sixteen-and-over certified film, but soon shrugged this off as being the least of my worries on that score were the authorities to get wind of our relationship. Exposing a minor to scenes of astronauts mutating into alien organisms threatening to engulf and destroy humanity would probably be one of the lesser charges.

It was raining when we stumbled out of the cinema into the darkness of Notting Hill Gate. Although there was no shortage of cafés there I jumped at Rosemarie's suggestion of Soho and music. I was slowly getting accustomed to the awareness that there was not much we could do to change the reality that in a week we would be several thousand miles apart and I wanted to find a place and a moment away from the mews to see if she shared the realism of that dismal view.

**The window poster for John Barry Seven guitarist
Keith Kelly dates this picture to 1959**

The *2i's* coffee bar got its name from the Irani brothers who owned the place. A dark steamy smoke-filled cellar beneath the café served as a music venue, Here it was the melody that was king. No fancy stage, just a couple of scaffold boards on upturned boxes to raise the night's musicians above the sixty or so who could crowd in. No amplification for the band, just an ancient microphone for the singer. Most times you never knew who was going to be performing, just whatever band was free that night. But there was never a night without the muffled beat of some rock and roll drummer greeting you as you walked up Old Compton Street. On nights when the smoke and sweat in the crowded basement at number 59 had reached saturation level one of the brothers would open the basement delivery doors and young people would gather beside them, jiving at no cost, not even a frothy coffee.

Old Compton Street Soho

A typical evening crowd. *The Heaven and Hell* at 57 was a coffee lounge next door to the *2i's*. No live music here, just two jukeboxes, one in Heaven (white-painted ground floor) one in Hell (totally black basement, with red flames and devil masks for lights). When the regulars tired of the juke box it was easy to tip in to the *2i's* next door. (Picture puzzle: Is that really someone making a mobile phone call in 1958?)

A dangerously overcrowded dump, but it epitomised the breakaway spirit of the fifties. We made our way into the café past the usual formica table tops and glass cups of the time, through the door at the back and down to the cellar on narrow steps I had trodden so many times.

Next morning, Rosemarie was no longer tearful. I had tried to be positive about America, land of opportunity and all that sort of stuff. In the *2i's,* when the volume allowed, we had agreed that what would be - would be and that after Christmas we would meet up come what may; but how convinced either of us were with the mutual deception was scarcely in doubt. Just a determination to enjoy sharing the immediate time ahead. Real-life was shouting at us like it does, but we were determined not to listen.

A week later Rosemarie left to join her parents in Texas and for a while our letters carried promises of meeting, but for teenagers the hands of time tracing such divided lives creep ever more slowly and gradually the letters became less frequent. Her studies, she wrote, occupied her more and more. For me the strident call of the buff envelope of the Royal Air Force also presaged a different life with different preoccupations for the next two years.

ೞಒ

Chapter sixteen

Epilogue

> "tis true that a good play needs no epilogue;
> good plays prove the better by the help of good epilogues"
> Rosalind in *As You Like It*
> William Shakespeare

London's Oxford Street has been a magnet for shoppers from the late Victorian times and especially since Mr Selfridge changed the capital's shopping habits with the arrival of his emporium in 1908. In those days another no less successful entrepreneur Thomas Tilling operated horse-buses from Oxford Street to Peckham on its route number 12. The Routemaster I was on one late October afternoon in the 1970s had retained the ancient route number though it bore scant resemblance to Mr Tilling's 34 seater. In the 1970s, in another remnant of Tilling's times, the stairs from the upper deck still descended at the rear of the bus on to an open platform for alighting.

From my seat in the back of the bus I idly observed a pair of legs clad in the sheerest stockings, descending. The hairs on the back of my neck stood up. Surely it couldn't be? Those legs, those unmistakable limbs could belong only to one person. The legs had paused and turned around as their owner addressed someone behind them. And then, descending further she was revealed. I rose and called to her and in an instant her face broke into the smile that had so eluded her when we had first met after her ordeal of the plane crash. Behind her a child of about seven years old, in straw hat surveyed me quizzically and took my hand and examined me with big blue enquiring eyes. Rosemarie did the introductions.
"This is Andrea." She drew out the middle syllable. "An_dre_a this is Terry."
"You know my Mommy?" The enquiry unmistakably American.
"Oh yes." I said, taking the child's extended hand.
"We're going to Hamberleys." She said, excitedly jumping up and down.
"Hamley's darling. I promised her, before we go back."
In a rush I found myself asking if they would have dinner with me but they were meeting Daddy and leaving early next day. I wanted to ask her so many things. When had she married? Were there other children? I wondered how she felt about flying and remembered her terror at the noise in the desert and her closeness.

The bus was slowing to their toy-shop stop. Wildly I asked for her address and she rummaged for a card unsuccessfully.
"We're at the Waldorf, ask the reception I'll tell them it's OK". The crowd was surging in and for a moment she was lost in the tumult. The pair alighted to be met by a tall man with cigar and white ten-gallon hat that cast a long shadow and hid his face in the setting sun.

The bus began its run down to the long curve that would take it into Piccadilly Circus to where the winged archer idly contemplated ventilating passing motorists. I sat there for a while as the bus rounded Trafalgar Square, my recollection an endless reel of pictures. My mind kept returning to the image of the Texan, his hat, his cigar. Was it all real? Then I recalled the final view.

The trio had been swallowed-up into the toy-store and a moment later the child had reappeared, waving. She took off her straw hat and it had fluttered vigorously shaking out her hair with the effort, the golden mane cascaded around her shoulders, catching the sunlight and set off by the bright red ribbon.

I never went to the Waldorf. There didn't seem much point. We were no more connected now than Mr Tilling's horse-bus and the big red Routemaster, except in rosy recollection. Life was like that; casual impulses that made lives collide and then move on. Long ago a moment in time had been given to us, but time and the moment had passed. Sahara to Soho, Picardy to Pinewood, truly these were the blue remembered hills, happy highways that cannot come again.

༺༻

Our revels now are ended. These our actors,
As I foretold you, were all spirits and
Are melted into air, into thin air
And like the baseless fabric of this vision
The cloud-capped tow'rs, the gorgeous palaces
The solemn temples, the great globe itself,
Yea all which it inherit, shall dissolve
And like this insubstantial pageant faded,
Leave not a rack behind. We are such stuff
As dreams are made on and our little life
Is rounded with a sleep.

Prospero. *The Tempest.* Act 4 Sc 1
William Shakespeare

ಸಿಳಿ

Capt. David Rhys Griffiths.

Pilots of No 10 (Sunderland) Squadron RAAF based at RAF Mountbatten, Plymouth, England operating with RAF Coastal Command in the Battle of the Atlantic. Seven of those pictured were later awarded DFCs. Five of the smiling faces never returned from the war.

P.O. (later Flt.Lt.) David Rhys Griffiths back row fourth left. A dozen years later, as a BOAC captain, the Air Accident Board found that the Argonaut accident in Tripoli was the result of the Captain's error of judgement. In his fourth attempt to land on the badly-lit runway using visual approach he failed to use flight instruments adequately. In the restricted visibility the runway lights gave him insufficient guidance as to attitude, height and angle of approach. Unknowingly he permitted the aircraft to descend below its correct approach path.

(Picture: Australian War Memorial collection)

BIBLIOGRAPHY

A Life to Remember
William MacQuitty
Quartet Books 1991

Empress of Ireland
Christopher Robbins
Scribener 2004

Gangland Bosses
J.Moreton & G.Parker
Time-Warner Books 2004

Golden Gong, The
Quentin Falk
Columbus Books 1987

Travelling the Road
Brian Desmond Hurst
Unpublished

ಸಿಂ

INDEX

(bold print = pictures)

007, 142 (see Bond.J)
12th Airforce 60
20th Century Fox 16
2i's coffee bar **167**-9
2LO radio 85
376 Heavy Bombardment 60

Above us the Waves 17, 18
Advertising, Early tv 6, 53, 163
Afrika Corps 15, 33
Alcott, Arthur 14
American Forces Radio and
   Television Service 63
Andrews, Revd Basil 120-1, 139
Andrews, Eamonn 102, **103**
Another Man's Poison 138
Archer Street 117
Argonaut 26-7, 29, 31, 64, 131-
   132,176
Argonaut DC4 crash
   Tripoli 26-29, 34, 35, 176
   Colorado 129
Astor, Lord 110
Attlee, Clement 99-**100**
ATS 131
AutoClub Tripoli 57
Aziza, Libya 51

Baddeley Cake 75-**76**
Baddeley, Robt 75
Bader, Douglas 146
Ball, Lucille   64
Ballet Russe   140
Barbary Fort, Tripoli 40, **41**
Battle of Frith Street 120
Battle of the River Plate 140
Bayswater 89, 92, 122-3
BBC Home Service, 129
Bedford, Duke of 108
Belfast Telegraph 5
Bernadette 161
Bert (crew) 32, 34-6, 49
Birkin, Sir Henry 59
Black Narcissus 44

Black Tent, The **23**, 137, 139, **149,150, back-cover**
BOAC 11, 12, 27, 130-2,176
Bogarde, Dirk 18, 137, 146, 148
Bond, James 159 (see 007)
Borzacchini, Mario U 59
Bow Street's Magistrates 3
Box, Sidney 18
*Boys from Syracuse, Th*e 140
Bradford Alhambra   73
Brigade of Guards 2
Bristol Superfreighter 152
British Eighth Army 15, 55
British Nat'l Films Company 4
Bronte family 109
Brook, Clive 18-19, 21,
Brooking, Dorothea 87
Brooking, Timothy 69,84-5.**87**
Bruno, Sgt (dog) **62**
Burston, Reginald 82

Caesar and Cleopatra 44
Canestrini, Giovani 56-7
Carousel 69
Carry Ons, 144-5
Casablanca 12
Casino, Le Touquet, 158-160
Casino Royale 159
Castel Benito, RAF 13
Charing Cross Hospital 120
Charisse, Cyd 33
Charm-school, (Rank) 18
Chartered Bank of India 5
Children and Young Pers Act 3
Christie,(mass murderer), 92
Christmas Carol, A 2
Churchill, Winston 99, 109
Ciampino airport 26
Cinemascope 16
Clapham College 78,125,**128**
Cliveden 110
Club Eleven 114-15
Closed-shop 77
Cole, Nat King 113
Collyer, Ken 115
Comer, Jack (Spot) **119**, 120,
Comer, Rita 120-2
Comet, 130-2
Court Players 81
Coward, Noel 154-5

Cowell, Simon 4
Creeping Unknown, 166
Crippen, Dr 3
Crosby, Bing 113
Crown Film Unit 18
Crown of Queen Victoria 5
Croydon Airport 81, 155
Cruel Sea, The 18
Cuffe Burton, Sir Wm. 131
Cy Laurie Jazz Club 115-6, 122, 124, 158-9,

Daily Sketch 121
Daly, David 141
DanAir 132
Dancing Years, The 75
Dangerous Moonlight 2
Davies,Js First Off 26,28
Davis, Bette 138
Davis, John 140, 144
Dawson, Beatrice 43
DC4 see argonaut
de Leon, Mary 163
DeHaviland Comet130-32
Denham Studios 18, 50
Denton, Geoffrey 69, 83, **87**, 114, 120, 122
Denville Hall 141
Denys-Burton, Sir C.P. 133-5
Denys-Burton, Eliz 135
Denys-Burton,Margaret 26-7 **130**-1, 133
Dickens, Charles 152
Dickinson, Desmond 50
Dietrich, Marlene 154
Differing, Anton 33
Dimes, Albert 119-20
Divorce, 134
Doctor films 18, 148
Draycott Hall 131
Drury Lane 6, 32, **67-70**, 75, -6, 80, 82, 85, 101-2, 104-5, 111, 112, 140
Duchess Theatre 101-2
Duke, Doreen 72-**74**
Dunkirk 160

Earls Court 141
Edward VII 5
Edward VIII 154-5

Ekberg, Anita 138-**41**
Eleven Club 113-4
Elizabeth II, Queen 131
Embassy Club 115,
Empire Theatre, L'pool 110
Enchanted Cottage, The vii
Entertainments National Service Association (ENSA) 18, 69, 104
Equity 71, 79
Eros 123, 125
Estelle, (Madame brothel) 5
Everyman Theatre L'pool 110

F86 Sabrejets 61
Fellini, Federico 141
Ferryfield 151
Fidelma (neighbour) 93,106
Finch, Peter 149
Fleming Ian 159
Flying Duchess 109
Flynn, Errol 40, 138
Ford. John 2
France, Dixie 122
Fred, (Drury Lane) 82
Frith Street 118, 120, 122

Gafara Plain 51
Gainsborough Studios 14
Galloway, Lennox Maj 133
Garrick, David 77
Gauldie, Wm 28, 129
George III 68
Ghaddafi 55
Ghibli 27, 52
Gibbons, Caroll 85
Glass shot 50
Goldie, (Dresser) 69, 80
Granger, Stewart 44
Great Expectations 152
Great Missenden 82, 145
Grenadier Guards 18
Griffiths, R.D.E Capt 26-29, **176**
Grimaldi, Joe 73
Gryspeerdt, Norman 150
Guardian, The 141

Hallam, Thomas 73
Ham Yard 114, 122, 124
Hamlet 50, 83
Hammer Films 166

179

Hammerstein, Oscar 69, 77, 79
Hangman's House 2
Hardcore 140
Harley Street 131
Harmony Inn cafe 117, 121
Hanson, Harry 81
Harvey, John 68-9, 70,72, **76**-79,81-3,**87**
Hawkins, Jack 137
Heartbreak Hotel 113
Heatherden Hall, (Pinewood) 144
Heathrow 11, 26, 151
Heaven and Hell cafe **168**
Heilebron, Rose QC 119
Hepburn, Audrey 153
Hermes aircraft 11, 12, 131
Hitler, Adolf 156
Hobson, Valerie 72, 75, 76,122
Hollywood 2, 17, 50,138-9 144-6
Horridge, Justice 134
House of all Nations brothel 5
Howarth, Yorks 109
Hudson, Rock 139
Hurst, Brian Desmond 2, 3,18-**21**, **23**, 52, 175
Hyde Park 81, 123, 144

I Love Lucy 64
Idris Airport 11-13, 26-28, 38, 61, 64, 176
Imperial Airways 132
Indecent Displays Act 118
Information, Min of 18
Irani Brothers 167
Irish Free State lottery, 56
Irving, Henry 77, 102
Ivory Hunter, The 139

Jaeger, Frederick 33
Jambo, 139
Jerome, Sister 124-5
John of Gaunt 75
Jones, Betty Jo 73
Joseph, Teddy 14

Kano, Nigeria 26
Karloff, Boris 97
Keeler, Christine 110
Kensal Green 121
Kerr, Deborah 44

King and I, The 6, **71**, 75, 85
Knight,Eddie 50
Kruschev, Nikita 61
Kubrick, Stanley 14

L'hirondelle 115
La Dolce Vita 141
Lagos, Nigeria 26, 28
Lanza, Mario 49
Laurie, Cy 115-**6**,, 122 124, 158-9
Lawrence of Arabia 40
le Neve, Ethel 3
Le Touquet 151-56,160
Leno, Dan 73-4
Lets Get Laid 140
Letter from Ulster 18
Libya, 13, 39, 41, 55
Lilley, Bea 18
Lister, Eve 75, **80**
Littleton, Humphrey 115
Liverpool,Western Approaches 109,
Liverpool Empire 110
Lom, Herbert **76**
London Evening News 4
London Melody 144
Lotterie dei Millioni 57
Lydd airport 149, 153
Lympne, Kent 151

Mac's Club 114-5
Mac's Dancing Acad'y 114
Macklin, Charles 73
MacQuitty, Wm 3, 5, 6, 8, 17, -19, **23**, 42, 51, 114, 146, 175
Mallaha race track 56-**59**
Malta Story, The 18
Man in Grey, 75
Manor at Northstead, The 101
Margaret iii, 26, 27, 129-33, 135
Margate 134
Martin, Ann 76
Martin, Mary 69,
Mary, (neighbour) 92-98 105-6
Master of Ballantrae 138
Matthews, A E 101-3
McKenna, Virginia 146
McQueen-Pope, W **104**-5
Mellaha Tripoli 56-60
Men of Two Worlds, 50

180

Messenger, Dudley 50
Methodist Times 4
MGM 17
Mix, Tom 77
Moffats Club 115
Monmouth, Duke of 117
Monroe, Marilyn 44
Montgomery,Fld/Marsh 15
More, Kenneth 146,
Morell, Andre **150**
Moss Bros 8
Murray, Barbara 138
Murrays Club 115, 134
Musician's Union 114
Mussolini, Benito 39, 41, 49, 56, 57
My Fair Lady 4

Neagle, Anna 146
New York ii, 138
Nigeria 12, 13, 26, 45, 164
Night To Remember, A 3
Northern Ireland, 18
Northwood 101, 141
Notting Hill Gate 81, 166
Novello, Ivor 75
Nuvolari, Tazio 59

Oklahoma 69, 72, 75
Old Bailey 119-21
Old Compton St. 118, 168
Old Vic 85
Olivier, Laurence 50, 54
Olrich, April 140
On Approval 8, 21
Oxford Street 120-1, 171

PanAm 130
Parachute Regiment 140
Paramount 16
Parry, Sir Herbert 78
Pathé 139
Peck, Gregory 141
Peterborough Rep 81
Picardy,Hotel 155-8, 160, 173
Piccadilly, 80, 103, 122-3, 149, 173
Picknett, Lynn 111
Pigalle 115
Pinewood Studios v. 14, 37 **143**-4
Piscine, Le (Brothel) 5
Pleasance, Donald 49

Popie, tv series 104
Powell, Taffy Air Cdre 152
Presley, Elvis 113
Prince and the Showgirl, 44
Prince Regent 68
Profumo, John 72, 75, 110
Provis, George 51

Quatermass Xperiment **166**
Quiet Man, The 2

RAAF 27, 176
RAF 13, 30, 35, 137, 156, 169, 176
Rains, Claude 12
Rank Charm School 18
Rank, J Arthur 3, 4, 8, 14, 17, 18, 30, 137, 139, 140, 144 -6
Rape of Malaya 146
Reach for the Sky 146
Religious Films Limited 4
Rivio, Enrico 58
Robe, The 16
Rodgers, Richard 69, 77, 79
Rome 26, 39, 130, 132, 140-1, 153
Rommel, Erwin 15, 33
Rosemarie 30, 32, 33, 34, 35, 39, 40, 41, 42, 43, 44, 45, 52, 60, 61, 63, 64, 65, 67, 69, 85, 113-18, 121-24,129, 149-55, 157-9, 164-7, 169, 172
Royal Air Force. see RAF
Royal Australian Air Force see RAAF
Royal Film Performance 139

Sabratha 31, 32, **33**, 34
Sahara v, 19, 23, 26, 32, 51, 52, 66, 145, 173
Sandri, Anna Maria 42, 49, **150**
Savoy 85, 86
Savoy Orpheans 85
Scott, Ronnie 114
Scrooge 2
Secret Submarines 5, 17
Selfridges 171
Sergeant Bruno 62
Sexual Offences Act 148
Shaftesbury Avenue 117, 122

181

Shakespeare, Wm   20, 75, 77,
   79, 171, 173
Sheriden, Dinah   37
Silver City Airways   151, **153**
Simba   18
Simpson, Wallis   154-5
Sinatra, Frank   113
Sinden, Donald   18, 20, 49, 138,
   149-51
Sketch, Daily   121
Smart, Charles   28
Smith, Alan Essler   150
Smith, Gerald   82,
Smith, Jimmy   70,
Soho   v, vi, 105, 114-18, 120-22,
   124, 158, 167-8, 173
South Africa Airways   132
South Pacific   69, 75
Spanish Gardner, The   146
Spot, Jack   **119**-21(See Comer)
St Martin's Art School   115
Stalin, Joseph   61
Steel, Anthony   17, 42, 137-**139**-42
Stephen, Brother 78
Storm over the Nile   137
Strand Electric   105
Street Offences Act   118
Suicide Squadron   2
Sunday Thoughts   4
Sunderland flying boat   27, 176

Taylor, Elizabeth. 147
Technicolor   v, 22, 50
Tennyson, Peggy   133
Theatre Royal,
   (see Drury Lane)
This is your Life   102
Thomas, Basil   81
Tiger Moth   108
Tilley, Iris   42
Tilling, Thomas   171, 173
Times, The   6, 138-9
Tom Brown's Schooldays   2
Town Like Alice, A   146
Tribe, Lady Mary   109
Tripoli   11, **12, 13**, 14, 18, 22, 26-7,
   31, 32, 39, **40**-2, 44, 50, 51, 55,
   57, 60, 63, 67, 83, 118, 120, 129,
   138, 158, 176

Tripoli, Grand Hotel,   iii, **14,** 25,
   67, 85

Underwater Fishermen   42
Unexplained, The   111
United Airlines   129
United Artists   17
Universal   17
Universe, Miss   138

Van Druten, John   77
Varzi, Achille   58, 59
Verity Films   18
Vistavision   17, 52
Vittorio Emanuele III   57

Waddan Hotel Tripoli   36
Walbrook, Anton   2
Wanger, Walter   147
Ward, Stephen   110
Warner Bros   138, 175
Waters, Jack   70, 75
Wayne, John   2
Webber, Andrew Lloyd   75
Western Approaches L'pool   109
Westgate Hotel Margate   134
Westminster, Duke of   2
Westminster Hotel Le Touquet
   154, 158, 160
Wheelus Army Air Field   iii, 34, 44,
   55, **60**, 62, 63, 64, 65
Where No Vultures Fly   139
Whiteleys   91
Wilde, Daryl   85
Windmill Theatre   83, 114, 117-8,
Winslow Boy, The   **128**
Wisdom, Norman   146
Woburn Abbey   108-9
Wodehouse, P.G.   155
Wolverhampton Grand   81
Wong, Anna May   7
Wooden Horse, The   18, 139

Young, Charles Mayne   84,

Back cover : Terence Sharkey and Donald Sinden. *The Black Tent*

By the same author

A tantalizing pursuit. Involves the reader.   *Birmingham Daily News.*

Several features recommend it. It is clear, concise and well organised. A lively account.   *Spectator.*

On balance the better (of two books reviewed). A chilling book to read beside a roaring coal fire.   *Daily Mail.*

Not all Ripper writers manipulate. Terence Sharkey has a porky Catholicity – his "pick your own Ripper" has all the cheerful openness of a welcoming fruit farm.   *Guardian.*

Other press comment included:

Builds a vivid picture of Victorian life.

A very interesting and absorbing book, not for the squeamish.

An amazing DIY guide.

Jack the Ripper
100 Years of Investigation
Ward Lock. London
Dorset Press. New York
Soon available in Kindle.

Printed in Great Britain
by Amazon

81581108R00112